"Nothing would have bee
the words of the title in tl
John Stott, not just reading ... Bible. For in his preaching
as in his writing, John Stott's greatest gift was to help people see and
hear clearly what the Bible itself actually says, and then, of course, to
challenge us as to how we should respond to what we see and hear. Not
all of us possess the complete works of John Stott. But we do possess
the complete Bible. These sensitively edited extracts from Stott's
writings will not only introduce new readers to the riches of his biblical
exposition (and make them hungry for more), but will surely also introduce them to riches of God's Word they had not seen before."

Christopher J. H. Wright, international ministries director,
Langham Partnership

"No one I have known has loved, preached, taught, and lived the Bible
any more than John Stott. He often quoted Spurgeon's comment that
we should seek for our very blood to become 'Bibline'; so seriously
should we soak in Scripture in order to know and live it. This new series
will give us daily help in just such living."

Mark Labberton, president, Fuller Theological Seminary, author of *Called*

"John Stott explains the Scriptures with a brilliant mind, a pastor's heart,
and a soul gripped by the beauty, glory, and love of Jesus."

Greg Jao, vice president and director of campus engagement,
InterVarsity Christian Fellowship

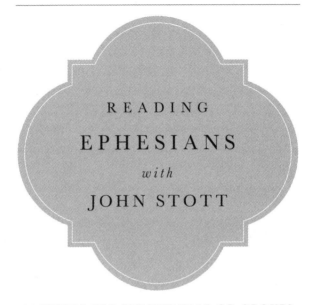

READING

EPHESIANS

with

JOHN STOTT

11 WEEKS FOR INDIVIDUALS OR GROUPS

JOHN STOTT

with ANDREW T. LE PEAU

IVP Connect

An imprint of InterVarsity Press
Downers Grove, Illinois

InterVarsity Press
P.O. Box 1400, Downers Grove, IL 60515-1426
ivpress.com
email@ivpress.com

This volume is abridged and edited from The Message of Ephesians ©1979 by John R. W. Stott, by
permission of Inter-Varsity Press, England. Some of the discussion questions are from Ephesians:
Building a Community in Christ ©1998 by John R. W. Stott with Phyllis J. Le Peau.

InterVarsity Press® is the book-publishing division of InterVarsity Christian Fellowship/USA®, a
movement of students and faculty active on campus at hundreds of universities, colleges, and
schools of nursing in the United States of America, and a member movement of the International
Fellowship of Evangelical Students. For information about local and regional activities, visit
intervarsity.org.

All Scripture quotations, unless otherwise indicated, are taken from the Holy Bible, New
International Version®, NIV®. Copyright © 1973, 1978, 1984, 2011 by Biblica, Inc.™ Used by
permission of Zondervan. All rights reserved worldwide. www.zondervan.com The "NIV" and
"New International Version" are trademarks registered in the United States Patent and Trademark
Office by Biblica, Inc.™

Cover design: Cindy Kiple
Interior design: Beth McGill
Images: © Mark Bauer / Trevillion Images

ISBN 978-0-8308-3195-1 (print)
ISBN 978-0-8308-9241-9 (digital)

Printed in the United States of America ♾

Library of Congress Cataloging-in-Publication Data
Names: Stott, John R. W., author.
Title: Reading Ephesians with John Stott : 11 weeks for individuals or groups
  / John Stott, with Andrew T. Le Peau.
Description: Downers Grove : InterVarsity Press, 2017. | Series: Reading the
  Bible with John Stott (RBJS)
Identifiers: LCCN 2017016290 (print) | LCCN 2017013140 (ebook) | ISBN
  9780830892419 (eBook) | ISBN 9780830831951 (pbk. : alk. paper)
Subjects: LCSH: Bible. Ephesians—Textbooks.
Classification: LCC BS2695.55 (print) | LCC BS2695.55 .S76 2017 (ebook) | DDC
  227/.50071—dc23
LC record available at https://lccn.loc.gov/2017016290

P	20	19	18	17	16	15	14	13	12	11	10	9	8	7	6	5	4	3	2	1
Y	33	32	31	30	29	28	27	26	25	24	23	22	21	20	19	18	17			

Contents

How to Read the Bible
with John Stott

During John Stott's life (1921–2011), he was one of the world's master Bible teachers. Christians on every continent heard and read John Stott's exposition of Scripture, which was at once instructive and inspiring. With over eight million copies of his more than fifty books sold in dozens of languages, it is not surprising that *Time* magazine recognized him in 2005 as one of the "100 Most Influential People in the World" and *Christianity Today* called him "evangelicalism's premier teacher and preacher." At the core of his ministry was the Bible and his beloved Bible Speaks Today series, which he originated as New Testament series editor. He himself contributed several volumes to the series, which have now been edited for this Reading the Bible with John Stott series.

The purpose of this series is to offer excerpts of Stott's *The Message of Ephesians* in brief readings, suitable for daily use. Though Stott was himself an able scholar, this series avoids technicalities and scholarly debates, with each reading emphasizing the substance, significance and application of the text.

Following each set of six readings is found a discussion guide. This can be used by individuals to help them dig more deeply into the text. It can also be used by study groups meeting regularly. Individuals in the groups can go through the readings between group meetings and then use the discussion guide to help the group understand and apply the Scripture passage. Discussions are designed to last between forty-five and sixty minutes. Guidelines for leaders at the end of this volume offer many helpful suggestions for having a successful meeting.

If you are a group member, you can help everyone present in the following ways:

1. Read and pray through the readings before you meet.

2. Be willing to participate in the discussion. The leader won't be lecturing. Instead all will be asked to discuss what they have learned.

3. Stick to the topic being discussed. The focus is the particular passage of Scripture. Only rarely should you refer to other portions of the Bible or outside sources. This will allow everyone to participate on equal footing.

4. Listen attentively to what others have to say. Be careful not to talk too much but encourage a balanced discussion among all participants. You may be surprised by what you can learn from others. Generally, questions do not have one right answer but are intended to encourage various dimensions of the text.

5. Expect God to teach you through the passage and through what others have to say.

6. Use the following guidelines and read them at the start of the first session.

- We will make the group a safe place by keeping confidential what is said in the group about personal matters.
- We will provide time for each person to talk who wants to.
- We will listen attentively to each other.
- We will talk about ourselves and our own situations, avoiding conversation about others.
- We will be cautious about giving advice to one another.

John Stott had an immense impact on the church in the last half of the twentieth century. With these volumes readers today can continue to benefit from the riches of the Bible that Stott opened to millions.

Introduction

❦

Ephesians is a marvelously concise yet comprehensive summary of the good news and its implications. Nobody can read it without being moved to wonder and worship, and challenged to consistency of life. The letter focuses on what God did through the work of Jesus Christ and what he does through his Spirit today in order to build his new society in the midst of the old.

It tells how Jesus Christ shed his blood in a sacrificial death for sin, was then raised from death by the power of God and has been exalted above all competitors to the supreme place in both the universe and the church. More than that, we who are "in Christ," united to him by faith, have ourselves shared in these great events. We have been raised from spiritual death, exalted to heaven, and seated with him there. We have also been reconciled to God and to each other. As a result, through Christ and in Christ, we are nothing less than God's new society, the single new humanity he is creating, which includes Jews and Gentiles on equal terms. We are the family of God the Father, the body of Jesus Christ his Son, and the temple or dwelling place of the Holy Spirit.

Therefore we are to demonstrate plainly and visibly by our new life the reality of this new thing God has done: first by the unity and diversity of our common life, second by the purity and love of our everyday behavior, next by the mutual submissiveness and care of our relationships at home, and last by our stability in the fight against the principalities and powers of evil. Then in the fullness of time God's purpose of unification will be brought to completion under the headship of Jesus Christ.

With this theme in mind, we may perhaps outline the letter as follows:

1. The new life God has given us in Christ (1:3–2:10)

2. The new society God has created through Christ (2:11–3:21)

3. The new standards God expects of his new society, especially unity and purity (4:1–5:21)

4. The new relationships into which God has brought us— harmony in the home and hostility to the devil (5:21–6:24)

The whole letter is thus a magnificent combination of Christian doctrine and Christian duty, Christian faith and Christian life, what God has done through Christ and what we must be and do in consequence. And its central theme is "God's new society."

This message of the church as God's new creation and new community is of particular importance for those of us who call ourselves or are called evangelical Christians. For by temperament and tradition we tend to be rugged individualists, and are thought to care little about the church. Indeed, the expressions "evangelical" and "low church" are generally supposed to be synonymous. Yet they should not be. True evangelicals, who derive their theology from the Bible, will be bound to have the very "high" view of the church that the Bible has. Today more than ever we need to catch the biblical vision of the church.

In the West the church is in decline and urgently needs to be renewed. But what form of renewal do we desire? In parts of the world the church is stripped of privilege, often persecuted, and sometimes driven underground. Such situations prompt the basic question: what is the church's essential being without which it would cease to be the church? Then in several regions of the Majority World the church is growing rapidly, and in some places its growth rate is faster even than the population growth rate. But what kind of churches are coming into being and growing? Thus in every part of the world we need to ask radical questions about the church. And Ephesians will supply us with answers.

John Stott

1

Ephesians 1:1-14
A Life of Spiritual Blessing

❦

Grace to You

EPHESIANS 1:1-2

¹Paul, an apostle of Christ Jesus by the will of God,

To God's holy people in Ephesus, the faithful in Christ Jesus:

²Grace and peace to you from God our Father and the Lord Jesus Christ.

Paul claims the same title Jesus had given to the Twelve, designating somebody specially chosen, called and sent to teach with authority. He had not volunteered for this ministry, nor had the church appointed him. On the contrary, his apostleship derived from the will of God and from the choice and commission of Jesus Christ. If this is so, then we must listen to the message of Ephesians with appropriate attention and humility.

The apostle then describes the readers of his letter as saints. He is not referring to some spiritual elite but to all God's people.

They were called "saints" (that is, "holy") because they had been set apart to belong to him. The expression was first applied to Israel as the "holy nation," but came to be extended to the whole international Christian community, which is the Israel of God (Galatians 6:16).

His initial message to them is one of grace and peace. *Grace* indicates God's free, saving initiative, and *peace* points to the initiative he has taken to reconcile sinners to himself and to each other in his new community. These are key words in Ephesians. So if we want a concise summary of the good news that the whole letter announces, we could not find a better one than the three monosyllables "peace through grace."

What then is the vital link between Paul, his readers, and his message? It is the Lord Jesus Christ himself. For Paul the author is "an apostle *of Christ Jesus*," the readers are themselves *in Christ Jesus*, and the blessing comes to them both from God our Father and from *the Lord Jesus Christ*, who are bracketed as the single spring from which grace and peace flow. Thus the Lord Jesus Christ dominates Paul's mind and fills his vision. It seems almost as if he feels compelled to bring Jesus Christ into every sentence he writes, at least at the beginning of this letter. For it is through and in Jesus Christ that God's new society has come into being.

The Past Blessing of Election

EPHESIANS 1:3-4

3Praise be to the God and Father of our Lord Jesus Christ, who has blessed us in in the heavenly realms with every spiritual blessing in Christ. [4]For he chose us in him before the creation of the world to be holy and blameless in his sight.

Paul stresses that the blessing God gives us in Christ is *spiritual*. A contrast is probably intended with Old Testament days when God's promised blessings were largely material. It is true Jesus promised his followers some material blessings, for he forbade them to be anxious about food, drink, and clothing, and assured them that their heavenly Father would supply their needs if they put the concerns of his rule and righteousness first.

Christians are trinitarians. We believe in one God, the Father, the Son, and the Holy Spirit. We affirm with gratitude and joy that God has blessed us in Christ with every spiritual blessing. That is, every blessing of the Holy Spirit has been given us by the Father if we are in the Son. No blessing has been withheld from us. Of course we still have to grow into maturity in Christ, be transformed into his image, and explore the riches of our inheritance in him. Of course, too, God may grant us many deeper and richer experiences of himself on the way. Nevertheless, if we are in Christ, every spiritual blessing is ours already.

Also note the statement "he chose us in him." God put us and Christ together in his mind. He determined to make us (who did not yet exist) his own children through the redeeming work of Christ (which had not yet taken place). It also arose from his entirely unmerited favor, since he chose us "to be holy and blameless before him." This means that when in his mind he chose us, we were unholy and blameworthy, and therefore deserving not of adoption but of judgment. So this is no cause for boasting.

Now everybody finds the doctrine of election difficult. "Didn't I choose God?" somebody asks, and we must answer, "Yes, indeed you did, and freely, but only because in eternity God had first chosen you." Scripture nowhere dispels the mystery of election, and we should beware of any who try to systematize it too precisely or rigidly.

The truth of God's election, however many its unresolved problems, should lead us to righteousness, not to sin; and to humble adoring gratitude, not to boasting. Its practical consequences should always be that we live on the one hand "holy and blameless in his sight" (v. 4) and on the other "to the praise of his glorious grace" (v. 6).

The Present Blessing of Adoption

EPHESIANS 1:5-8

> [5]He predestined us for adoptions to sonship through Jesus Christ, in accordance with his pleasure and will— [6]to the praise of his glorious grace, which he has freely given us in the One he loves. [7]In him we have redemption through his blood, the forgiveness of sins, in accordance with the riches of God's grace [8]that he lavished on us.

When people ask us why God went ahead with the creation when he knew that it would be followed by the fall, one answer we can tentatively give is that he destined us for a higher dignity than even creation would bestow on us. He intended to adopt us, to make us the sons and daughters of his family. In Roman law (part of the background to Paul's writing) adopted children enjoyed the same rights as natural children. The New Testament has much to say about this status of sonship, its rich privileges and demanding responsibilities.

Take our privilege first. God's children enjoy a free access to their heavenly Father, and their confidence before him is due to the knowledge that they have been redeemed and forgiven. *Redemption* means "deliverance by payment of a price." Here it is equated with forgiveness, for the deliverance in question is a rescue from the just judgment of God on our sins, and the price paid was the shedding of Christ's blood when he died for our sins on the cross. So redemption, forgiveness, and adoption all go together. We become his sons and daughters because of the lavish outpouring of his grace on us.

But adoption implies responsibility too, for the heavenly Father does not spoil his children. On the contrary, he "disciplines us for our good, in order that we may share in his holiness" (Hebrews 12:10). So Paul's two statements are parallel, that "he destined us . . . to sonship" (v. 5) and "he chose us . . . to be holy" (v. 4). It is inconceivable that we should enjoy a relationship with God as his children without accepting the obligation to imitate our Father and cultivate the family likeness.

So then adoption as God's sons and daughters brings both a plus and a minus, an immense gain and a necessary loss. We gain access to him as our Father through redemption or forgiveness. But we lose our blemishes, beginning at once by the sanctifying work of the Holy Spirit, until we are finally made perfect in heaven. What seems to unite the privilege and the responsibility of our adoption is the expression "in his sight" (v. 4) or "in his presence." For to live our life in the conscious presence of our Father is both an immeasurable privilege and a constant challenge to please him.

The Future Blessing of Unification

Ephesians 1:9-10

> [9]He made known to us the mystery of his will according to his good pleasure, which he purposed in Christ, [10]to be put into effect when the times reach their fulfillment—to bring unity to all things in heaven and on earth under Christ.

God has done more than choose us in Christ in a past eternity and give us sonship now as a present possession. He has also "made known to us the mystery of his will" for the future. This is "purposed in Christ, to be put in effect when the times reach their fulfillment."

History is neither meaningless nor purposeless. It is moving toward a glorious goal. God's plan "when the times reach their fulfillment," when time merges into eternity again, is "to bring unity to all things in heaven and on earth under Christ." Already Christ is head of his body, the church, but one day "all things" will acknowledge his headship. At present there is still discord in the universe, but in the fullness of time the discord will cease, and the unity we long for will come into being under the headship of Jesus Christ.

What are the "all things" which will one day be united under Christ? Certainly they include the Christian living and the Christian dead, the church on earth and the church in heaven.

No doubt angels will be included too. But "all things" normally means the *universe*, which Christ created and sustains. So Paul seems to be referring to that cosmic renewal, that regeneration of the universe, that liberation of the groaning creation. In the fullness of time, God's two creations, his whole universe and his whole church, will be unified under the cosmic Christ, who is the supreme head of both.

If we shared the apostle's perspective, we would also share his praise. For doctrine leads to doxology as well as to duty. Life would become worship, and we would bless God constantly for having blessed us so richly in Christ.

We Who Hoped in Christ

EPHESIANS 1:11-12

[11]In him we were also chosen, having been predestined according to the plan of him who works out everything in conformity with the purpose of his will, [12]in order that we, who were the first to put our hope in Christ, might be for the praise of his glory.

The spiritual blessings Paul has been describing belong equally to Jewish and Gentile believers. The structure of the paragraph makes this plain: "In him we [Jews], who were the first to put our hope in Christ. . . . When you [Gentiles] believed you were marked in him with a seal" (vv. 12-13). Paul is anticipating his theme of the reconciliation of Jews and Gentiles, which will come in chapter 2. Christ is the reconciler. Through union with Christ the people of God are one.

Paul is alluding to the church as God's inheritance and possession. These words used to be applied exclusively to the nation of Israel but are now reapplied to an international people whose common factor is that they are all in Christ. How did this happen? We became God's people or possession neither by chance nor by choice (that is, by our choice). Rather it was by God's own sovereign will and pleasure.

Why then did God make us his people? "For the praise of his glory." This beautiful phrase needs to be unpacked. The glory of God is the revelation of God, and the glory of his grace is his self-disclosure as a gracious God. To live to the praise of the glory of his grace is both to worship him ourselves by our words and deeds as the gracious God he is, and to cause others to see and to praise him too. This was God's will for Israel in the Old Testament days, and it is also his purpose for his people today.

Such a perspective comes into violent collision with the human-centeredness and self-centeredness of the world. Fallen humanity, imprisoned in its own little ego, has an almost boundless confidence in the power of its own will, and an almost insatiable appetite for the praise of its own glory. But the people of God have at least begun to be turned inside out. The new society has new values and new ideals. For God's people are God's possession who live by God's will and for God's glory.

You Who Heard the Truth

EPHESIANS 1:13-14

[13]And you also were included in Christ when you heard the message of truth, the gospel of your salvation. When

you believed, you were marked in him with a seal, the promised Holy Spirit, [14] who is a deposit guaranteeing our inheritance until the redemption of those who are God's possession—to the praise of his glory.

Although Paul attributes our salvation entirely to the will of God, in the same context he describes our own responsibility. We "heard the message of truth," which is also called "the gospel of . . . salvation." Then we "believed" and were sealed with "the promised Holy Spirit." Let no one say that the doctrine of election by the sovereign will and mercy of God, mysterious as it is, makes either evangelism or faith unnecessary. The opposite is the case. It is only because of God's gracious will to save that evangelism has any hope of success and faith becomes possible. The preaching of the gospel is the very means God has appointed by which he delivers from blindness and bondage those he chose in Christ.

We are assured that God is active in the lives of his people through the Holy Spirit, who is given three designations—promise, seal, and guarantee. First, he is literally the Spirit of the promise because God promised through the Old Testament prophets and through Jesus to send him (which he did on the Day of Pentecost), and God promises to give him today to everyone who repents and believes (which he does).

Second, the Holy Spirit is God's seal, a mark of ownership and authenticity. Cattle, and even slaves, were branded with a seal by their masters in order to indicate who they belonged to. But such seals were external, while God's is in the heart. He puts his Spirit within his people to mark them as his own.

Third, the Holy Spirit is God's guarantee to bring his people safely to their final inheritance. In ancient commercial transactions, a guarantee signified a first installment or down payment. In this case the guarantee is not something separate from what it guarantees but actually the first portion of it. An engagement ring promises marriage, but is not itself a part of the marriage. A deposit on a house is more than a guarantee of payment; it is itself the first installment of the purchase price. So it is with the Holy Spirit. In giving him to us, God is not just promising us our final inheritance but actually giving us a foretaste of it.

Ephesians 1:1-14

....

DISCUSSION GUIDE

OPEN

How does being a part of Christian community help you to see God at work?

STUDY

Read Ephesians 1:1-14.

1. What information does the introduction to this letter give (vv. 1-2)?

2. Much of the message of Ephesians is embedded in the apostle's opening salutation: "Grace and peace to you from God our Father and the Lord Jesus Christ" (v. 2). What is the significance of the emphasis on grace and peace?

3. We are told in verse 3 that we are blessed with "every spiritual blessing in Christ." Carefully list each of the blessings in verses 4-8.

4. As you reflect on these blessings, what contributions do you see of each person of the Trinity—the Father, the Son,

and the Holy Spirit? (Although the Holy Spirit is mentioned by name only in verses 13 and 14, his activity is assumed throughout.)

5. How do these blessings relate to the past (v. 4), the present (v. 7), and the future (v. 10)?

6. How are you affected by the fact that God had a plan for you before the world was created?

7. What is this purpose of God for the future (v. 10)?

8. What do you think it will mean to have all things under the head of Christ?

9. In verses 11-14 it seems that Paul is alluding to the church as God's "inheritance" and "possession." These words used to be applied exclusively to the nation of Israel but are now reapplied to an international people whose common factor is that they are all "in Christ." The fact that the same vocabulary is used of both peoples indicated the spiritual continuity between them. How did we become God's possession (vv. 5, 9, 11-12)?

10. How does it feel to think of yourself as God's inheritance and possession?

11. Describe the Holy Spirit and his role in fulfilling this purpose of God (vv. 13-14).

12. Notice the repeated phrase "to the praise of his glory" in verses 5-6, 12, 14. What does it mean to live "to the praise of his glory"?

APPLY

1. How does your life need to change so that you are living to the praise of God's glory?

2. How can you influence your Christian community to live for God's glory?

3. In silence reflect on all that we have in Christ Jesus. Praise God for each and all of the spiritual blessings he has given to you—past, present, and future. Ask the Holy Spirit to make them a reality in your life.

Ephesians 1:15-23
A Life of Prayer

❦

Blessing and Intercession

EPHESIANS 1:15-17

[15]For this reason, ever since I heard about your faith in the Lord Jesus and your love for all God's people, [16]I have not stopped giving thanks for you, remembering you in my prayers. [17]I keep asking that the God of our Lord Jesus Christ, the glorious Father, may give you the Spirit of wisdom and revelation, so that you may know him better.

Although Paul is naturally thinking of his readers he is writing to, throughout the first chapter of his letter he addresses himself to God instead of to them. He begins with a great benediction (vv. 3-14) and continues with a great intercession (vv. 15-23).

For a healthy Christian life it is important that we follow Paul's example and keep Christian praise and Christian prayer together. Yet many do not preserve this balance. Some Christians seem to do little but pray for new spiritual blessings, apparently oblivious of the fact that God has already blessed them in Christ with every spiritual blessing. Others lay such emphasis on the truth that everything is already theirs in Christ that they become complacent and appear to have no appetite to know or experience their Christian privileges more deeply. Both groups must be declared unbalanced. They have created a polarization that Scripture will not tolerate.

In Ephesians 1 Paul encourages us to both keep praising God that in Christ all spiritual blessings are ours and to keep praying that we may know the fullness of what he has given us. If we keep together praise and prayer, benediction and petition, we are unlikely to lose our spiritual equilibrium.

As we continue to compare the two halves of Ephesians 1, another feature strikes us: both are essentially trinitarian. Both are addressed to God the Father, the benediction to "the God and Father of our Lord Jesus Christ" (v. 3), and the intercession to "the God of our Lord Jesus Christ" (v. 17), who is also called "the glorious Father." Next, both refer specifically to God's work in and through Christ, for on the one hand he "has blessed us . . . in Christ" (v. 3) and on the other he accomplished in Christ a mighty act of power when he resurrected and enthroned him (v. 20). Third, both sections of the chapter allude—even if obliquely—to the work of the Holy Spirit, since the blessings God bestows on us in Christ are "spiritual" blessings (v. 3), and it is only by "the Spirit of wisdom and of revelation" that we can come to know them (v. 17).

Christian faith and Christian life are both fundamentally trinitarian. And the one is a response to the other. Because the Father has approached us in blessing through the Son and by the Spirit, we can approach him in prayer through the Son and by the Spirit also.

Knowing God

> [15]For this reason, ever since I heard about your faith in the
> Lord Jesus and your love for all God's people, [16]I have not
> stopped giving thanks for you, remembering you in my
> prayers. [17]I keep asking that the God of our Lord Jesus
> Christ, the glorious Father, may give you the Spirit of
> wisdom and revelation, so that you may know him better.

What prompts Paul to launch into prayer for his readers is
something he had heard about them. In the previous paragraph
he has written in fairly general terms how he and his fellow
Jewish Christians "were the first to put our hope in Christ"
(v. 12) and how his readers as Gentile believers had "heard the
message of truth" and believed in Christ (v. 13). Now he becomes
more personal: "I heard about your faith in the Lord Jesus and
your love for all God's people." This is why Paul says he continuously thanks God for them and then encompasses them
with his prayers. For despite his unceasing gratitude to God for
them, he is still not satisfied with them.

So what is his request? It is not that they may receive a
"second blessing" but rather that they may appreciate to the
fullest possible extent the implications of the blessing they have
already received. So the essence of his prayer for them is "that
you may know" (v. 18). We must not overlook this emphasis.
Growth in knowledge is indispensable to growth in holiness.
Indeed, knowledge and holiness are even more intimately linked
than as means and end. For the "knowledge" Paul prays for is

more Hebrew than Greek in concept; it adds the knowledge of experience to the knowledge of understanding. More than this, it emphasizes knowing him (v. 17), knowing God personally, as the context within which we "may be enlightened" (v. 18), that is, may come to know truths about him. There is no higher knowledge than the knowledge of God himself.

Such knowledge is impossible without revelation. So Paul prays that God "may give you the Spirit of wisdom and revelation, so that you may know him better" (v. 17). We do not ask God to "give" the Holy Spirit himself to those who have already received him and been "marked in him with a seal" (v. 13), but rather that we may and should pray for his ministry of illumination. Because of his confidence in this ministry of the Spirit, Paul can continue his prayer: "that the eyes of your heart may be enlightened in order that you may know. . . ." In biblical usage the heart is the whole inward self, comprising mind as well as emotion. So the eyes of the heart are simply our inner eyes, which need to be opened or enlightened before we can grasp God's truth.

The Hope of God's Call

EPHESIANS 1:18

18I pray that the eyes of your heart may be enlightened in order that you may know the hope to which he has called you, the riches of his glorious inheritance in his holy people.

The call of God takes us back to the very beginning of our Christian lives. "Those he predestined, he also called; those he called, he also justified" (Romans 8:30). True, we called on him to save us, but our call was a response to his (Romans 10:12-13).

The question now is: What did God call us for? His call was not a random or purposeless thing. He called us to something and for something. And it is this that is meant by "the hope of his call" (v. 18, literally). It is the expectation we enjoy as a result of the fact that God has called us.

The rest of the New Testament tells us it is a rich and varied expectation. For God has called us "to belong to Jesus Christ" and "into the fellowship with . . . Jesus Christ" (Romans 1:6; 1 Corinthians 1:9). He has called us "to be his holy people" and "to a holy life," since he who has called us is holy himself. (Romans 1:7; 1 Corinthians 1:2; 2 Timothy 1:9). One of the characteristics of the holy or special people of God is liberation from the judgment of God's law, for we were "called to be free" (Galatians 5:1, 13). Another characteristic is harmonious fellowship across the barriers of race and class, for we "as members of one body . . . were called to peace" (Colossians 3:15; Ephesians 4:1-2).

At the same time, though we may enjoy peace within the Christian community, we are bound to experience opposition from the unbelieving world. Yet we must not retaliate: "To this [unjust suffering and patient endurance] you were called, because Christ suffered for you, leaving you an example, that you should follow in his steps" (1 Peter 2:21). Besides, we know that beyond the suffering lies the glory. For God has also called us "to his eternal glory in Christ."

All this was in God's mind when he called us. He called us to Christ and holiness, to freedom and peace, to suffering and glory.

More simply, it was a call to an altogether new life in which we know, love, obey, and serve Christ, enjoy fellowship with him and with each other, and look beyond our present suffering to the glory that will one day be revealed. This is "the hope to which he has called you." Paul prays that our eyes may be opened to know it.

The Glory of God's Inheritance

EPHESIANS 1:18

¹⁸I pray that the eyes of your heart may be enlightened in order that you may know the hope to which he has called you, the riches of his glorious inheritance in his holy people.

The apostle's second prayer to God is that we may know "the riches of his glorious inheritance in his holy people." The Greek expression, like the English, could mean either God's inheritance or ours, that is, either the inheritance he receives or the inheritance he bestows. Some commentators take it in the first sense and understand it to refer to the inheritance God possesses among his people. Certainly the Old Testament authors taught consistently that God's people were his inheritance or possession, and we found a reference to this truth in verses 12 and 14. But the parallel passage in Colossians 1:12 strongly suggests the other interpretation here, namely, that God's inheritance refers to what he will give us, for we are to give thanks to the Father, "who has qualified you to share in the inheritance of his holy people in the kingdom of light."

In this case, if God's call points back to the beginning of our Christian life, God's inheritance points on to its end, to that final inheritance of which the Holy Spirit is the guarantee (v. 14) and which Peter says "can never perish, spoil or fade [that] is kept in heaven for you" (1 Peter 1:4). For God's children are God's heirs, in fact "co-heirs with Christ" (Romans 8:17), and one day by his grace the inheritance will be ours. Exactly what it will be like is beyond our capacity to imagine. So we are wise not to be too dogmatic about it. Nevertheless certain aspects of it have been revealed in the New Testament, and we will not go wrong if we hold fast to these. We are told that we will see God and his Christ, and worship him; that this beatific vision will be a transforming vision, for "when Christ appears, we shall be like him," not only in body but in character; and that we will enjoy perfect fellowship with each other. For God's inheritance (the inheritance he gives us) will not be a little private party for each individual but rather among God's holy people as we join that "great multitude that no one could count, from every nation, tribe, people and language, standing before the throne and before the Lamb" (1 John 3:2; Philippians 3:21; Revelation 7:9).

Paul does not regard it as presumptuous that we should think about our heavenly inheritance or even anticipate it with joy and gratitude. On the contrary, he prays that we may know it, the glory of it, indeed, "the riches of his glorious inheritance."

The Greatness of God's Power

EPHESIANS 1:18-23

[18]I pray that the eyes of your heart may be enlightened in order that you may know the hope to which he has called

you, the riches of his glorious inheritance in his holy
people, [19]and his incomparably great power for us who
believe. That power is the same as the mighty strength [20]he
exerted when he raised Christ from the dead and seated
him at his right hand in the heavenly realms, [21]far above
all rule and authority, power and dominion, and every
name that is invoked, not only in the present age but also
in the one to come. [22]And God placed all things under his
feet and appointed him to be head over everything for the
church, [23]which is his body, the fullness of him who fills
everything in every way.

If God's call looks back to the beginning and God's inheritance
looks on to the end, then surely God's power spans the interim
period in between. How will we come to know the surpassing
greatness of the power of God? First, by Jesus Christ's resurrection from the dead.

Death is a bitter and relentless enemy. It will come to all of
us one day. While we may succeed in postponing death, we
cannot escape it. And after death nothing can stop the process
of decay and decomposition. Even the most sophisticated em-
balming techniques of modern morticians cannot preserve the
body forever. No. We are dust, and to dust we shall inevitably
return (Genesis 3:19). No human power can prevent this, let
alone bring a dead person back to life.

But God has done what no one else can do. He raised Jesus
Christ from the dead. First, he arrested the natural process of
decay, refusing to allow his Holy One to see corruption (Acts
2:27). Then he did not just reverse the process, restoring the dead

Jesus to this life, but he raised Jesus to an altogether new life (immortal, glorious, and free), which nobody had ever experienced before and nobody has experienced since—or not yet.

Second, God "made him sit at his right hand in the heavenly realms" (v. 20). That is, he promoted him to the place of supreme honor and executive authority. In doing so, he fulfilled the messianic promise of Psalm 110:1: "The LORD says to my lord: 'Sit at my right hand until I make your enemies a footstool for your feet.'" With God's power Christ reigns in absolute supremacy over all.

We come to know the surpassing greatness of the power of God through the resurrection of Christ and by seating Christ at his right hand (vv. 19-21). But there is a third way. He is appointed "head over everything for the church." These three belong together. Because of Christ's resurrection from the dead and enthronement over the powers of evil, he has been given headship over the church, which he fills in every way. The one that God gave to the church to be its head was already head of the universe. Thus both universe and church have in Jesus Christ the same head.

The Unity of Knowledge and Faith

EPHESIANS 1:15-23

> [15]For this reason. . . . [17]I keep asking that the God of our Lord Jesus Christ, the glorious Father, may give you the Spirit of wisdom and revelation, so that you may know him better. [18]I pray that the eyes of your heart may be

enlightened in order that you may know the hope to which he has called you, the riches of his glorious inheritance in his holy people, [19]and his incomparably great power for us who believe.

The whole thrust of Paul's prayer is that his readers may have a thorough knowledge of God's call, inheritance, and power, especially the latter. But how did he expect his prayer to be answered? How do Christians grow in understanding? Some say that knowledge depends on the enlightenment of the Holy Spirit. And they are right, at least in part. For Paul prays that "the Spirit of wisdom and revelation" may increase their knowledge of God and enlighten the eyes of their hearts. We have no liberty to infer from this, however, that our responsibility is solely to pray and to wait for illumination, and not to do the work of thinking. Others make the opposite mistake: they use their minds and think, but leave little room for the enlightenment of the Holy Spirit.

Paul brings the two together. First, he prays that the eyes of his readers' hearts may be enlightened to know God's power. Then he teaches that God has already supplied historical evidence of his power by raising and exalting Jesus. Thus, God has revealed his power objectively in Jesus Christ and now illumines our minds by his Spirit to grasp this revelation. Divine illumination and human thought belong together.

Many assume that faith and reason are incompatible. This is not so. The two are never contrasted in Scripture, as if we had to choose between them. Faith goes beyond reason but rests on it. Knowledge is the ladder by which faith climbs higher.

So Paul prayed "that you may know . . . [what is the] incomparably great power for us who believe" that he accomplished in Christ (vv. 18-19). It is vital to see how Paul brings together the verbs *to know* and *to believe*. The resurrection power God exhibited in Christ is now available for us. First, we are to know its surpassing greatness as demonstrated in Christ's resurrection and enthronement, and then we are to lay hold of it experimentally for ourselves by faith. Thus knowledge and faith need each other. Faith cannot grow without a firm basis of knowledge; knowledge is sterile if it does not bring forth faith.

The very same power of God has raised us with Jesus from spiritual death and enthroned us with Jesus in heavenly places (Ephesians 2:1-10). But how much of this is theory, and how much is experience? It is not difficult to think of our human weakness: our tongue or our temper, malice, greed, lust, jealousy, or pride. These things are certainly beyond our power to control. And we have to humble ourselves to admit it. But are our weaknesses beyond the power of God? No. The power of God that raised Jesus from the dead and raised us with him has put all things under his feet. So it can put all evil under ours as well.

Ephesians 1:15-23

Discussion Guide

Open

In what ways do you struggle to maintain a consistent life of prayer and praise?

Study

Read Ephesians 1:15-23.

1. How would you describe the tone of these verses?

2. What motivates Paul to pray for the Ephesians?

3. List the requests he makes for them in this prayer.

4. Why would the "Spirit of wisdom and revelation" (v. 17) help the Ephesians to know God better?

5. What does it mean to "know" God?

6. In biblical usage the heart is the whole inward self, comprising mind as well as emotion. What do you think it means to have "the eyes of your heart ... enlightened" (v. 18)?

7. The call of God takes us back to the very beginning of our Christian lives. "Those he predestined, he also called; those

he called, he also justified" (Romans 8:30). Think about what it is to be called by God. Why is this a source of hope for us?

8. God's inheritance points to the end of our lives, to that final inheritance of which the Holy Spirit is the guarantee (v. 14). Based on what you know from the New Testament, describe this glorious inheritance.

9. Describe God's incomparably great power according to verses 19-22.

10. Why are the resurrection and ascension such a vivid demonstration of divine power?

11. What would it look like to see that power at work in the church today?

APPLY

1. In what ways would you like to know God better?

2. In what ways do you have difficulty bringing faith and knowledge together?

3. What difference would it make in your life if your eyes were more opened to the hope of God's call?

4. The church is central to God's plan (vv. 22-23). What role does the church play in your life?

5. Pray the content of this prayer for your church, yourself, and one other Christian friend.

Ephesians 2:1-10
A Life of Resurrection

❧

The Human Condition

EPHESIANS 2:1-3

> [1]As for you, you were dead in your transgressions and sins, [2]in which you used to live when you followed the ways of this world and of the ruler of the kingdom of the air, the spirit who is now at work in those who are disobedient. [3]All of us also lived among them at one time, gratifying the cravings of our flesh and following its desires and thoughts. Like the rest, we were by nature deserving of wrath.

Just before this passage Paul had prayed that his readers' inward eyes might be enlightened by the Holy Spirit to know the implications of God's call to them and the surpassing greatness of his power that is available for them (1:15-23). Ephesians 2, then, is really a part of Paul's prayer that they (and we) might know God's power to raise the dead. Its first few words emphasize this: "you were dead." The sequence of thought is clear: Jesus Christ was dead, but God raised and exalted him. And you also were dead, but God raised and exalted you with Christ.

In this devastating portrayal of the human condition apart from God in these first three verses of chapter two, Paul is describing everybody. He is not giving a picture of some particularly decadent tribe or degraded segment of society. No, this is the biblical diagnosis of fallen people in fallen society everywhere. True, Paul begins with an emphatic *you*, indicating in the first place his Gentile readers in Asia Minor, but he quickly goes on to write that "all of us also lived" in the same way (thus adding himself and his fellow Jews), and he concludes with a reference to the rest of humankind (2:3). Here then is a condensation into three verses of the first three chapters of Romans, in which he argues his case for the sin and guilt first of pagans, then of Jews, and so of all humanity.

I sometimes wonder if good and thoughtful people have ever been more depressed about the human predicament than they are today. Of course every age is bound to have a blurred vision of its own problems because it is too close to them to get them into focus. And every generation breeds new prophets of doom. Nevertheless, the pervasiveness of the media enables us to grasp the worldwide extent of contemporary evil in ways not possible before, and this is what makes the modern scene look so dark.

Partly this is due to the escalating economic problems (hunger, periodic economic crises, the abuse of natural resources, multigenerational poverty among certain groups), partly the spread of social conflict (racism, tribalism, class struggle, terrorism, disintegrating family life) and partly the absence of accepted moral guidelines (leading to violence, dishonesty, and sexual promiscuity). We seem incapable of managing our own affairs or of creating a just, free, humane, and tranquil society. This all deserves our prayer, time, and resources. But Paul also reminds us that we must not lose sight of this: humanity itself is askew.

We Were Dead

EPHESIANS 2:1-3

> [1]As for you, you were dead in your transgressions and sins, [2]in which you used to live when you followed the ways of this world and of the ruler of the kingdom of the air, the spirit who is now at work in those who are disobedient. [3]All of us also lived among them at one time, gratifying the cravings of our flesh and following its desires and thoughts. Like the rest, we were by nature deserving of wrath.

The death Paul refers to is not a figure of speech, as is the case in the parable of the prodigal son: "This son of mine was dead." Rather it is a factual statement of everybody's spiritual condition outside of Christ. And it is traced to their "transgressions and sins." These two words seem to have been carefully chosen to give a comprehensive account of human evil. The Greek for a transgression is a false step, involving either the crossing of a known boundary or a deviation from the right path. A sin, however, means missing the mark or falling short of a standard. Together the two words cover the positive and negative, or active and passive, aspects of human wrongdoing. That is, our sins of commission and of omission. Before God we are both rebels and failures. As a result, we are dead or "separated from the life of God" (Ephesians 4:18). For true life, eternal life, is fellowship with the living God, and spiritual death is the separation from him that sin inevitably brings.

This biblical statement about the deadness of non-Christian people raises problems for many because it does not seem to square with the facts of everyday experience. Lots of people who make no Christian profession whatever, who even openly repudiate Jesus Christ, appear to be very much alive. One has the energetic body of an athlete, another the lively mind of a scholar, a third the vivacious personality of a film star. Are we to say that such people, if Christ has not saved them, are dead? Yes, indeed. We must and do say this very thing.

In the sphere that matters supremely (which is neither the body nor the mind, nor the personality, but the soul) they have no life. And you can tell it. They are blind to the glory of Jesus Christ and deaf to the voice of the Holy Spirit. They have no love for God, no sensitive awareness of his personal reality, no leaping of their spirit toward him in the cry "Abba, Father," no longing for fellowship with his people. They are as unresponsive to him as a corpse.

So we should not hesitate to affirm that a life without God (however physically fit and mentally alert the person may be) is a living death, and that those who live it are dead even while they are living. To affirm this paradox is to become aware of the basic tragedy of fallen human existence.

The World, the Flesh, and the Devil

EPHESIANS 2:1-3

¹As for you, you were dead in your transgressions and sins, ²in which you used to live when you followed the ways of this world and of the ruler of the kingdom of the air, the spirit who is now at work in those who are disobedient. ³All of us also lived among them at one time, gratifying the cravings of our flesh and following its desires and thoughts. Like the rest, we were by nature deserving of wrath.

If behind death lies sin, what lies behind sin that holds us in such captivity? Paul refers to three influences as controlling and directing our former pre-Christian existence.

First, he describes us as having "followed the ways of this world." The Greek phrase is literally "according the age of this world." It brings together the two concepts of this present age of evil and darkness and of this world organized without reference to God. So both words *age* and *world* express a social value system alien to God. It dominates societies and holds people in captivity.

Wherever human beings are being dehumanized—by political oppression, human greed, or bureaucratic tyranny, by a secular, amoral, or materialistic outlook; by poverty, hunger, or unemployment, by racial discrimination, or by any form of injustice—there we find the subhuman values of this age and this world. People tend to surrender to the culture. It is a cultural bondage. We were all the same until Jesus liberated us.

The second captivity was to the devil—"the ruler of the kingdom of the air." The whole phrase need mean no more than that he has command of those spiritual powers who operate in the unseen world. "The spirit who is now at work in those who are disobedient" is another way of referring to Satan and his forces.

The third influence that holds us in bondage is "the cravings of our flesh" (v. 3). *Flesh* does not mean the fabric that covers our skeleton but our fallen, self-centered human nature. Its passions are further defined as "its desires and thoughts." This reference to our minds shows the error of equating "the cravings of our flesh" with what are popularly called the sins of the flesh. These sins include the wrong desires of the *mind* as well as of the *body*, namely, such sins as intellectual pride, false ambition, rejection of known truth, and malicious or vengeful thoughts. Wherever *self* rears its ugly head against God, there is "the flesh." Our ingrained self-centeredness is a horrible bondage.

A clarification: there is nothing wrong with natural bodily desires, whether for food, sleep, or sex. For God has made the human body that way. It is only when the appetite for food becomes gluttony, for sleep becomes sloth, and for sex becomes lust that natural desires have been perverted into sinful desires.

We cannot conveniently shift all the blame for our slavery on to the world, the flesh, and the devil. We must also accept responsibility. We are ourselves identified as "those who are disobedient" (v. 2). We had rebelled, knowingly and voluntarily, against the loving authority of God and so had fallen under the dominion of Satan.

We Were Condemned

EPHESIANS 2:3

> ³All of us also lived among them at one time, gratifying the
> cravings of our flesh and following its desires and thoughts.
> Like the rest, we were by nature deserving of wrath.

Paul has one more unpleasant truth to tell us about ourselves.
Not only were we dead and enslaved, he says, but we were also
condemned: "Like the rest, we were by nature deserving of
wrath." I doubt if there is an expression in Ephesians which
has provoked more hostility than this, so we must clear up two
key misconceptions.

First, God's wrath is not like ours. It is not bad temper, spite,
malice, animosity, or revenge. It is never arbitrary, since it is the
divine reaction to only one situation, namely, evil. God's wrath is
his personal, righteous, constant hostility to evil, his settled refusal
to compromise with it, and his resolve instead to condemn it.

Further, his wrath is not incompatible with his love. The contrast between verses 3 and 4 is notable: "We were by nature
deserving of wrath. But because of his great love for us, God,
who is rich in mercy . . ." Thus Paul is able to hold them together
in his mind because he believed they were held together in
God's character.

The second problem is in the adverbial clause "by nature,"
which raises the difficult questions about our genetic inheritance,
and therefore about our moral responsibility. Is Paul's phrase
shorthand for saying that by birth we have a tendency to sin,
that we therefore do sin, and that our sin brings us under the

judgment of God? Or is he saying that our very being as humans is from birth under God's judgment?

Probably the best commentary is Paul's own. Just as these verses are a condensed version of Romans 1–3, so the expression "by nature deserving of wrath" is a summary of Romans 5:12-14. His argument there that "death came to all people, because all sinned" is not that all inherited a sinful nature that led them to sin and so to die, but that "all sinned" in and with Adam. Hebrews 7:10 (RSV) speaks of the next generation as being already "in the loins" of the present generation, a truth which modern genetics may be said to underline. We were ourselves in Adam. It may truly be said that we sinned in Adam, and that in and with him we incurred guilt and died.

Our failure to recognize the gravity of the human condition explains people's naive faith in superficial remedies. Universal education is highly desirable. So are just laws administered with justice. Both are pleasing to God who is the Creator and righteous Judge of all. But a radical disease requires a radical remedy. We will not on that account give up the quest either for better education or for a more just society. Instead we will add evangelism, for God has entrusted to us a message of good news that offers life to the dead, release to the captives, and forgiveness to the condemned.

What God Did

EPHESIANS 2:4-7

> [4]But because of his great love for us, God, who is rich in mercy, [5]made us alive with Christ even when we were dead

in transgressions—it is by grace you have been saved. [6]And God raised us up with Christ and seated us with him in the heavenly realms in Christ Jesus, [7]in order that in the coming ages he might show the incomparable riches of his grace, expressed in his kindness to us in Christ Jesus.

We must hold both parts of this contrast together, namely, what we are by nature and what we are by grace. Christians are sometimes criticized for being morbidly preoccupied with their sin and guilt. The criticism is not fair when we are facing the facts about ourselves, but only when we fail to go on to glory in God's mercy and grace.

In one word he has *saved* us. In both verses 5 and 8 the same assertion is made: "By grace you have been saved." Paul is saying, "You are people who have been saved and remain forever saved." Because many find traditional salvation language meaningless, we need to probe more deeply.

Paul coins three verbs, which take up what God did to Christ and then link us to Christ in these events. First, God "made us alive with Christ" (v. 5), next he "raised us up with Christ" (v. 6), and third, he "seated us with him in the heavenly realms in Christ Jesus" (v. 6). These verbs (*made alive, raised*, and *seated*) refer to the three successive historical events in the saving career of Jesus, which are normally called the resurrection, the ascension, and the session. What excites our amazement, however, is that now Paul is not writing about Christ but about us. He is affirming not that God quickened, raised, and seated Christ, but that he quickened, raised, and seated us with Christ.

Fundamental to New Testament Christianity is this concept of the union of God's people with Christ. What constitutes the distinctness of the members of God's new society? Not just that they admire and even worship Jesus. No, what makes them distinctive is our new solidarity as a people who are "in Christ." By virtue of our union with Christ, God has blessed his people in Christ in the unseen world of spiritual reality (1:3), and there he has seated us with Christ (2:6). For if we are seated with Christ in the heavenly realms, there can be no doubt what we are sitting on: thrones!

This talk about solidarity with Christ in his resurrection and exaltation is not a piece of meaningless Christian mysticism. It bears witness to a living experience, that Christ has given us on the one hand a new life (with a sensitive awareness of the reality of God, and a love for him and for his people) and on the other a new victory (with evil increasingly under our feet). We were dead, but have been made spiritually alive and alert. We were in captivity, but have been enthroned.

Why God Did It

EPHESIANS 2:4-10

[4]But because of his great love for us, God, who is rich in mercy, [5]made us alive with Christ even when we were dead in transgressions—it is by grace you have been saved. [6]And God raised us up with Christ and seated us with him in the heavenly realms in Christ Jesus, [7]in order that in the coming ages he might show the incomparable riches of his grace, expressed in his kindness to us in Christ Jesus. [8]For

it is by grace you have been saved, through faith—and this is not from yourselves, it is the gift of God—[9]not by works, so that no one can boast. [10]For we are God's handiwork, created in Christ Jesus to do good works, which God prepared in advance for us to do.

Paul goes beyond a description of God's saving action; he tells us why God did it. Indeed the major emphasis of this whole paragraph is that what prompted God to act on our behalf was not something in us (some supposed merit) but something in himself (his own unmerited favor).

Paul assembles four ways to express God's motivation. He writes of God's mercy (v. 4), of God's love (v. 4), of God's grace (vv. 5, 8) and of God's kindness (v. 7). We were dead and helpless to save ourselves: so only mercy could reach us, for mercy is love for the down and out. We were under God's wrath: so only love could triumph over wrath. We deserved nothing at God's hand but judgment, on account of our trespasses and sins: so only grace could rescue us from what we deserve, for grace is undeserved favor. Why then did God act? Out of his sheer mercy, love, grace, and kindness.

In raising and exalting Christ he demonstrated "incomparably great power" (1:19-20), but in raising and exalting us he displayed also "the incomparable riches of his grace," and will continue to do so throughout eternity (2:7). As living evidences of his kindness we point people away and beyond ourselves to him to whom we owe our salvation.

Paul adds two balancing negatives to this depiction: it is neither our achievement ("not from yourselves" [v. 8]) nor a reward for any of your deeds of religion or philanthropy ("not by works" [v. 9]). This whole event and experience of being saved by God's grace through faith is God's free gift.

Finally, Paul adds one more positive, decisive, and glorious affirmation in verse 10. We are God's handiwork—or as F. F. Bruce has put it, "his work of art, his masterpiece." Salvation is creation, re-creation, new creation. And creation language is nonsense unless there is a Creator; self-creation is a patent contradiction in terms.

Some critics have supposed that Paul's doctrine of salvation by grace alone actually encourages us to continue in sin. They are entirely mistaken. Good works are indispensable to salvation— not as its ground or means, however, but as its consequence and evidence. We are not saved *because of works* (vv. 8-9), but we are created in Christ Jesus *for good works* (v. 10).

The contrast is complete between two lifestyles (evil and good), and behind them two masters (the devil and God). What could possibly have effected such a change? Just this: a new creation by the grace and power of God. That is the true meaning of salvation.

Ephesians 2:1-10

....

Discussion Guide

Open

What do you think life would be like for you right now if you had not become a Christian?

Study

Read Ephesians 2:1-10.

1. What were the Ephesians like before they met Christ?

2. What symptoms of being "dead in transgressions and sins" do you see in those you know who are not Christians?

3. Before Jesus Christ set us free, we were subject to oppressive influences from both within and without. To what forces are non-Christians enslaved (vv. 2-3)?

4. How have you seen these forces at work?

5. What does it mean to be objects of God's wrath?

6. In contrast to the desperate fallen condition of human beings, what three things has God done for us?

7. What do we learn about God's desires for us from these verses?

8. What does it mean to be "made alive with Christ" (v. 5)?

9. What are the implications of being "raised up with Christ," of being seated with him "in the heavenly realms"?

10. Why does Paul work so hard to make it crystal clear that this salvation is by grace, not our works or human effort?

11. How does Paul move our salvation from "it" to being intimately personal in verse 10?

12. Based on what you have seen in this passage, how would you explain what salvation is?

Apply

1. Christians are sometimes criticized for being morbidly preoccupied with their sin and guilt. The criticism is not fair when we are facing the facts about ourselves (for it is never unhealthy to look reality in the face), but only when we fail to go on to glory in God's mercy and grace. How do you respond to God's marvelous grace as you see it described here and experience it in your life?

2. How does this passage help you to point others away from yourself and toward God?

3. What hinders you from doing the good works God prepared for you to do?

4. Spend a few moments reflecting on your spiritual condition before you met Christ. Now praise him for the work of grace that he has done in you.

4

Ephesians 2:11-22

A New Humanity

❧

The Portrait of an Alienated Humanity

EPHESIANS 2:11-12

> [11]Therefore, remember that formerly you who are Gentiles by birth and called "uncircumcised" by those who call themselves "the circumcision" (which is done in the body by human hands)—[12]remember that at that time you were separate from Christ, excluded from citizenship in Israel and foreigners to the covenants of the promise, without hope and without God in the world.

For Jews in Paul's day, the world was sharply divided between Jews and Gentiles. Jews (the circumcised) scornfully called non-Jews "the uncircumcised." Circumcision had been given by God to Abraham as the outward sign of membership of his covenant people. But both the physical rite and the word had come to assume an exaggerated importance.

Paul declares the unimportance of names and labels in comparison with the reality behind them. Behind what is called the circumcision "done in the body by human hands" there is another kind, a circumcision of the heart, spiritual not physical, which was needed by and available to both Jews and Gentiles alike.

Gentiles, however, had more serious problems than most Jews realized. First, they "were separate from Christ."

The Gentiles' second and third disabilities were similar to one another. They were both "excluded from citizenship in Israel" and "foreigners to the covenants of the promise" (referring probably to the foundational promise made by God to Abraham). Israel was a nation under God, but the Gentiles were excluded.

The fourth and fifth Gentile disabilities are starkly stated: they were "without hope" and "without God in the world." Although God had planned and promised to include them one day, they did not know it, and therefore had no hope to sustain them. And they were godless because, although God had revealed himself to all humans in nature and therefore had not left himself without witness, they suppressed the truth and turned to idolatry (Romans 1:18-23), and they had no true knowledge of God and no personal fellowship with him.

We ourselves in our pre-Christian days were in exactly the same plight. We rebelled against the authority of God and knew little of true human community. Is it not the same in today's world without Christ? We still construct barriers of race, color, caste, tribe, or class. Divisiveness is a constant characteristic of every community without Christ.

Now the apostle says, "Therefore, remember," and again, "remember" (vv. 11, 12). There are some things Scripture tells us to forget (like the injuries that others do to us). But there is one thing in particular we are commanded to remember and never to forget—what we were before God's love reached down and found us. Only if we remember our former alienation will we be able to remember the greatness of the grace that forgave and is transforming us.

The Portrait of the Peacemaking Christ

EPHESIANS 2:13-14

> [13]But now in Christ Jesus you who once were far away have been brought near by the blood of Christ. [14]For he himself is our peace, who has made the two groups one and has destroyed the barrier, the dividing wall of hostility.

Both halves of Ephesians 2 begin with a description of life without Christ: dead (vv. 1-3) and separated (vv. 11-12). Then in both cases we have the great reversal: "But . . . God" (v. 4) and "But now" (v. 13). The main distinction is that in the second half Paul is stressing the Gentile experience.

The spatial language Paul uses in verse 13 (*far* and *near*) to describe the difference Christ made was not uncommon in the Old Testament. God and Israel were known to be near one another, since God had promised to be their God and to make them his people (Deuteronomy 4:7). By contrast, the Gentile nations were distant peoples who had to be summoned from afar (Isaiah 49:1).

Verse 13 contains two important additional references to Christ. "The blood of Christ" (as in 1:7) signifies his sacrificial death for our sins on the cross, by which he reconciled us to God and to each other, whereas "in Christ Jesus" signifies our personal union with Christ today through which the reconciliation he achieved is received and enjoyed.

Thus the two expressions witness to the two stages by which those far off are brought near. The first is the historical event of the cross, and the second is Christian conversion, or the contemporary experience of union with Christ.

The apostle goes on in verse 14 to elaborate the work of Christ in terms both of what he did and of how he did it. Christ Jesus shed his blood on the cross and offers himself to his people today to be united to them. He is now the peacemaker between us and with God. While the two groups, Jews and Gentiles, are reconciled in Christ, there is more. "The dividing wall of hostility" that symbolized Gentile alienation from God as well as from Israel has been destroyed by Christ.

Though the wall surrounding the temple, and still excluding the Gentiles, remained while Paul was writing this letter, spiritually it had already been destroyed when Jesus died on the cross.

This nearness to God that all Christians enjoy through Christ is a privilege we too frequently take for granted. Our God does not keep his distance, nor does he insist on any complicated ritual or protocol. On the contrary, through Jesus Christ and by the Holy Spirit we have immediate access to him as our Father (2:18). We need to exhort one another to avail ourselves of this privilege.

Something Old Abolished, Something New Created

EPHESIANS 2:15

¹⁵by setting aside in his flesh the law with its commands and regulations. His purpose was to create in himself one new humanity out of the two, thus making peace.

What did Christ do when he died on the cross to get rid of the divisive enmity between Jew and Gentile, between people and God? He *set aside*, *created*, and *reconciled*.

Christ broke down the wall, the hostility, "by setting aside in his flesh the law with its commands and regulations." This is a surprising statement. How can the apostle declare that Christ abolished the law when Christ himself specifically declared that he had not come to abolish it but to fulfill it (Matthew 5:17)?

In the Sermon on the Mount Jesus was referring to the *moral* law. He was teaching the difference between Pharisaic righteousness and Christian righteousness, advocating that Christian righteousness involves a deep and radical obedience to the law. Paul's primary reference in Ephesians seems to be to the *ceremonial* law "with its commands and regulations," that is, to circumcision (v. 11), the material sacrifices, the dietary regulations, and the rules about ritual cleanness and uncleanness that governed social relationships. They erected a serious barrier between Jews and Gentiles, but Jesus set this whole ceremonial dimension aside. And he did it "in his flesh" (surely a reference to his physical death), because in the cross he fulfilled all the Old Testament ceremonial system.

Paul is likely making another reference, this time to the moral, not the ceremonial, law. Jesus certainly did not abolish the moral law as a standard of behavior, but he did abolish it as a way of salvation. Whenever the law is viewed in this light it is divisive, for we cannot obey it, however hard we try. Therefore it separates us from God and from each other. But Jesus perfectly obeyed the law in his life, and in his death bore the consequences of our disobedience. Acceptance with God is now through faith in Christ crucified, whether for Jews or for Gentiles.

Paul then moves from the abolition of something old to the creation of something new. Jews and Gentiles were alienated from and at enmity with one another. But once the divisive law had been set aside, there was nothing to keep the two parts of humanity apart. Instead Christ created "one new humanity . . . thus making peace." This new humanity comes into existence and grows only by personal union with Christ.

In other passages Paul says that this new unity also does away with gender and social distinctions. "There is neither Jew nor Gentile, neither slave nor free, nor is there male and female, for you are all one in Christ Jesus" (Galatians 3:28). The facts of human differentiation are not removed. Men remain men and women, women; Jews remain Jews and Gentiles, Gentiles. But inequality before God is abolished. There is a new unity in Christ.

Peace and Access

EPHESIANS 2:16-18

[16]and in one body to reconcile both of them to God through the cross, by which he put to death their hostility. [17]He came and preached peace to you who were far away

and peace to those who were near. [18]For through him we
both have access to the Father by one Spirit.

In verse 16 we see the third verb describing how Christ's death
eliminated the divisive enmity between Jew and Gentile: *to reconcile* by putting to death the hostility that exists mutually between
God and people. It is not just that our attitude to him has been
one of rebellion but also that his wrath has been on us for our sin
(v. 3). And only through the cross have both hostilities been
brought to an end, for when Christ bore our sin and judgment on
the cross God turned away his own wrath, and we, seeing his great
love, turned away ours also. The hostility in both directions having
been decisively dealt with, the result is reconciliation.

This does not mean that the whole human race is now united
and reconciled. There is a further stage in the work of Christ that
Paul goes on to mention. Christ "came and preached peace"
(v. 17). Already we have been told that he is our peace (v. 14) and
that he created a new humanity, so making peace (v. 15). But now
he preached peace, publishing abroad the good news of the
peace he had made through the cross.

Although reconciliation is an event; access is the continuing
relationship to which it leads (v. 18). The Greek word for *access*
conjures up the scene in an ancient court, when subjects are
granted an audience with the king or emperor, and are presented
to him. The flavor of the word remains, but the emphasis changes
because our access is not to a king but to a Father, who "we may
approach . . . with freedom and confidence" (3:12).

Our access is "through him" (the Son who made peace and
preached it), "to the Father by one Spirit." Jews *and* Gentiles,

who as members of God's new society, now approach our Father together.

That is the vision. But when we turn from the ideal portrayed in Scripture to the concrete realities experienced in the church today, it is a very different and a very tragic story. For even in the church there is often alienation, disunity, and discord. Christians erect new barriers in place of the old.

I wonder if anything is more urgent today than that the church should be what by God's purpose and Christ's achievement it already is—a single new humanity, a model of human community, a family of reconciled brothers and sisters who love their Father and love each other, the evident dwelling place of God by his Spirit. Only then will the world believe in Christ as Peacemaker. Only then will God receive the glory due to his name.

God's Kingdom and God's Household

EPHESIANS 2:19

> [19]Consequently, you are no longer foreigners and strangers, but fellow citizens with God's people and also members of his household.

Paul has explained step by step what Christ has done to bring near to God and to his people those in the Gentile world who were previously far off. Christ has abolished the law of commandments, created a single new humanity in place of the two, reconciled both to God, and preached peace to those near and far. *Consequently*, what is the result of Christ's achievement and announcement of peace? This: "You [Gentiles] are no longer [what you used to be] foreigners and strangers," visitors without legal rights. On the contrary, your status has dramatically changed. Now you belong in a way you never did before.

To indicate the richness of their changed position and their new privileges in Christ, Paul resorts to familiar models of the church, which are developed in many other passages of Scripture. According to verse 12 the Gentiles used to be stateless and disenfranchised outsiders. But now, he calls them, "fellow citizens with God's people."

Although Paul does not develop the metaphor, he appears to be alluding to citizenship of God's kingdom. The kingdom of God is neither a territorial jurisdiction nor even a spiritual structure. God's kingdom is God himself ruling his people and bestowing on them all the privileges and responsibilities that his rule implies. To this new international God-ruled community, Gentiles and Jews belong on equal terms.

Paul is writing while the Roman Empire is at the zenith of its splendor. No signs had yet appeared of its coming decline. Yet he sees this other kingdom, neither Jewish nor Roman but international and interracial, as something more splendid and more enduring than any earthly empire. And he rejoices in this citizenship more even than in his Roman citizenship. Its citizens enjoy the stability of being a part of God's new society.

Paul now turns to a second image to describe the church: God's family. The metaphor becomes more intimate: "You are ... members of his [God's] household." In Christ, Jews and Gentiles find themselves more than fellow citizens under his rule;

they are together children in his family. Paul has just written in the previous verse of the new and privileged access to the Father that Jews and Gentiles enjoy through Christ (v. 18), and earlier in the letter he has enlarged on the blessings of adoption into his family (1:5).

Soon Paul will have more to say about God's archetypal fatherhood (3:14-15) and about the "one God and Father of all" (4:6), but here his emphasis seems to be less on God's fatherhood than on the brotherhood (meaning "brothers and sisters"), across racial barriers that the Father's children are brought into. This kind of familial love should be a special characteristic of God's new society.

God's Temple

EPHESIANS 2:19-22

> [19]Consequently, you are ... [20]built on the foundation of the apostles and prophets, with Christ Jesus himself as the chief cornerstone. [21]In him the whole building is joined together and rises to become a holy temple in the Lord. [22]And in him you too are being built together to become a dwelling in which God lives by his Spirit.

Paul first pictured the one new humanity as God's kingdom, and then as God's family. Now he likens it to the temple.

The temple in Jerusalem had for nearly a thousand years been the focal point of Israel's identity as the people of God. Now there was a new people who were not a new nation but a new humanity, international and worldwide. A geographically localized center would therefore not be appropriate for it. What then could be its temple, its focus of unity?

Nothing is more important to any edifice than a stable foundation. Paul says the church is "built on the foundation of the apostles and prophets" (v. 20). Since apostles and prophets both had teaching roles, it seems clear that what constitutes the church's foundation is neither their person nor their office but their instruction.

The word *apostles* here cannot therefore be a generic term for missionaries, church planters, bishops, or other church leaders. Instead it must denote that small and special group Jesus chose, called, and authorized to teach in his name, and who were eyewitnesses of his resurrection. What they taught they expected the church to believe and preserve; what they commanded they expected the church to obey.

The word *prophets* also indicates inspired teachers to whom the word of God came and who conveyed that word to others faithfully. Paul probably meant New Testament prophets. If so, the reference must be to a small group of inspired teachers, associated with the apostles, who together bore witness to Christ and whose teaching was derived from revelation (3:5). In practical terms this means that the church is built on the New Testament Scriptures.

The cornerstone is also of crucial importance to a building. It helps to hold the building steady, and it also sets it and keeps it in line. "The chief cornerstone" of the new temple is "Christ Jesus himself."

Paul moves on to the temple's individual stones: "In him you too are being built together." In Paul's picture, the extra stones ("you too") being built into the structure are the Gentiles. But now Gentiles are not only admitted; they are themselves constituent parts of the building. And since one of the cornerstone's functions was to bind two walls together, it may be that Paul is using this imagery to set Christ forth as the key to Jewish-Gentile solidarity.

What is the purpose of the new temple? In principle, it is the same as the old, namely, "to become a dwelling in which God lives" (v. 22). The new temple, however, is a spiritual building and an international community, and it has a worldwide spread. This is where God dwells. He is not tied to holy buildings but to holy people, to his own new society.

Ephesians 2:11-22

....

DISCUSSION GUIDE

OPEN

As you think about the church, what examples of divisions come to mind?

STUDY

Read Ephesians 2:11–22.

1. Trace the spiritual biography of the Gentiles in this passage.

2. What did Jesus do for the Gentiles?

3. As you think about individual Christians or groups of Christians that you separated from (because of theological, cultural, denominational, racial, or economic differences), what positive steps might you begin to take to heal these divisions?

4. How did Jesus bring the Jews and Gentiles together?

5. What is the significance of the fact that Jesus "preached peace to you who were far away and peace to those who were near" (v. 17)?

6. What does it mean to have access to the Father through one Spirit (v. 18)?

7. The status of the Gentiles has dramatically changed. Instead of being refugees they now have a home. What is the final outcome of Christ's destroying the wall of hostility (vv. 19-22)?

8. Think about this spiritual building that is being constructed. How are the apostles and prophets the foundation?

9. Why is Jesus considered the chief cornerstone of this building?

10. How do you respond to being a part of God's new society, built together into a holy temple in which God lives?

APPLY

1. How does this passage encourage you about your relationship with God and with other believers?

2. How might you take for granted being near to God?

3. What role do you think you might have in breaking down barriers between yourself and others?

4. Praise God for bringing you so close to himself and to other believers when at one time you were so far away. Ask him to work in you his grace to live out the truth that the dividing wall of hostility is down between all believers.

5

Ephesians 3:1-21
A New Ministry

❦

The Prisoner of Christ

> ¹For this reason I, Paul, the prisoner of Christ Jesus for the sake of you Gentiles—

Paul turns the attention of his readers away from themselves to himself, explaining his unique role in God's purposes for the Gentiles.

In the second half of Ephesians 2 he painted a vivid contrast between the double alienation the Gentiles endured before Christ (from God and from Israel) and their double reconciliation through Christ. For by his death Christ demolished both barriers, creating in relation to himself a single, new multicultural human society, which is both the family God loves and the temple he lives in. Paul's Gentile readers must have read with joyful amazement this exposition of the gospel of peace.

Now he styles himself as "the prisoner of Christ Jesus." Humanly speaking, he was not Christ's prisoner but Nero's. He had appealed to the emperor, and so to the emperor he had been committed for trial (Acts 25:11-12). But Paul believed in the sovereignty of God over human affairs. He was convinced that the whole of his life, including his wearisome imprisonment, was under the lordship of Jesus.

He then adds a second descriptive phrase. He was Jesus Christ's prisoner "for the sake of you Gentiles." This was a matter of fact. What had led to his arrest in Jerusalem, his imprisonment there and in Caesarea, his successive trials, and his subsequent appeal to Caesar (which had brought him to Rome) was fanatical Jewish opposition to his mission to the Gentiles. What prompted the Jews to stir up the crowd against Paul was his reputation for teaching "everyone everywhere against our people and our law and this place" (that is, the temple [Acts 21:28]).

How can he have acquired such a reputation? Doubtless by teaching exactly what he has just taught in Ephesians 2, namely, that by abolishing the divisive elements of the law Jesus was creating a new people and building a new temple. So he was arrested. And when the tribune allowed him to make his public defense to the Jewish people, they listened to him quietly until he got to the point in his story where Jesus had said to him: "Go; I will send you far away to the Gentiles." At this they shouted, "Rid the earth of him! He's not fit to live!" (Acts 22:21-22).

He not only preached his vision of the new and undivided humanity and wrote about it; he was at that moment suffering for the very truths he was expounding. No wonder he has come to be known as the apostle to the Gentiles.

The Mystery Made Known

EPHESIANS 3:2-6

²Surely you have heard about the administration of God's grace that was given to me for you, ³that is, the mystery made known to me by revelation, as I have already written briefly. ⁴In reading this, then, you will be able to understand my insight into the mystery of Christ, ⁵which was not made known to people in other generations as it has now been revealed by the Spirit to God's holy apostles and prophets. ⁶This mystery is that through the gospel the Gentiles are heirs together with Israel, members together of one body, and sharers together in the promise in Christ Jesus.

The way Paul describes his ministry here emphasizes the unique privileges God had given him in the outworking of his purpose for the Gentiles. Three times Paul uses the word *mystery* (vv. 3, 4, 9). In English a mystery is something dark, obscure, secret, puzzling. What is mysterious is inexplicable, even incomprehensible. However, the Greek word *mystērion* is different.

Originally, the Greek word referred to a truth someone had been initiated into. But in Christianity there are no esoteric mysteries reserved for a spiritual elite. On the contrary, the Christian mysteries are truths which, although beyond human discovery, have been revealed by God and so now belong openly to the whole church.

What is the particular open secret or revealed truth, "which was not made known to people in other generations" but "has now been revealed by the Spirit to God's holy apostles and prophets" (v. 5)? He spells it out in the next verse: "This mystery is that through the gospel the Gentiles are heirs together with Israel, members together of one body, and sharers together in the promise in Christ Jesus." Paul hammers home the point with three emphatic blows: Gentile and Jewish Christians together are now fellow heirs of the same blessing, fellow members of the same body, and fellow partakers of the same promise. And this shared privilege is both "in Christ Jesus" (because it is enjoyed equally by all believers, whether Jews or Gentiles, provided that they are in union with Christ) and "through the gospel" (because the gospel proclamation includes this unity and so makes it available to those who believe).

This double union, with Christ and with each other, is the substance of the mystery. It was a new revelation. For it was "not made known to people in other generations" (v. 5) but "which for ages past was kept hidden" (v. 9).

These statements have puzzled Bible readers because the Old Testament did reveal that God had a purpose for the Gentiles. It promised, for example, that all the families of the earth would be blessed through Abraham's posterity, that the Messiah would receive the nations as his inheritance, that Israel would be given as a light to the nations, and that one day the nations would make a pilgrimage to Jerusalem and even stream to it like a mighty river (Genesis 12:1-3; Psalm 2:8; Isaiah 2:2-4; 42:6; 49:6). Jesus also spoke of the inclusion of the Gentiles and commissioned his followers to go and make them his disciples.

What neither the Old Testament nor Jesus revealed was the radical nature of God's plan, which was that Jews and Gentiles would be incorporated into Christ and his church on equal terms without any distinction. What God revealed to Paul, this complete union of Jews, Gentiles, and Christ, was radically new.

The Dimensions of Paul's Ministry

EPHESIANS 3:7-10

> [7]I became a servant of this gospel by the gift of God's grace given me through the working of his power. [8]Although I am less than the least of all the Lord's people, this grace was given me: to preach to the Gentiles the boundless riches of Christ, [9]and to make plain to everyone the administration of this mystery, which for ages past was kept hidden in God, who created all things. [10]His intent was that now, through the church, the manifold wisdom of God should be made known to the rulers and authorities in the heavenly realms.

Paul has virtually equated the mystery with the gospel. The mystery was essentially truth revealed *to* Paul, while the gospel was essentially truth proclaimed *by* Paul. The privileged ministry of spreading the gospel he now elaborates in three stages.

Paul was commissioned first "to preach to the Gentiles the boundless riches of Christ" (v. 8). They are riches freely available because of the cross.

The second stage of Paul's privileged ministry he expresses in these terms: "to make plain to everyone the administration of this mystery, which for ages past was kept hidden in God, who created all things" (v. 9).

This verse does not simply repeat verse 8. There are three significant differences. First, the preaching of the gospel is now defined not as announcing good news but as enlightening the minds of people. We ourselves must always remember that our evangelism is the means God has ordained to bring light to those in darkness. A second difference lies in Paul's description of his message. According to verse 8 Paul's message was Christ; according to verse 9 it was the church. A final difference is that while Paul directs his ministry in verse 8 to Gentiles, in the next verse it is to everyone. The mystery includes the great promise that finally God will unite all things in and under Christ.

The third phase of Paul's ministry broadens "to the rulers and authorities in the heavenly realms" (v. 10). What does he mean? They are the cosmic intelligences, spectators of the drama of salvation.

Our knowledge of these spiritual beings is limited, and we must be careful not to go beyond what Scripture teaches. It is clear, however, that they are not omniscient. Similarly, we may infer from verse 10 that God had not revealed to them directly his master plan for the church, but intended rather to make it known to them *through the church* itself, as it came into being and grew.

These three different phases reveal the circle of divine communication: the good news was passed from God to Paul, from Paul and others to all humanity, and from the church on earth back to heaven again, to the cosmic powers. At each stage the medium changes. It is by direct revelation that God disclosed his plan to Paul, by the verbal proclamation of the gospel that the message spreads today, and by a visual model (the multicultural Christian community) that it finally reaches the unseen angelic spectators. Nothing is more honoring to the gospel, or more indicative of its surpassing importance, than this program for its universal communication.

The Centrality of the Church

EPHESIANS 3:10-13

> ¹⁰His intent was that now, through the church, the manifold wisdom of God should be made known to the rulers and authorities in the heavenly realms, ¹¹according to his eternal purpose that he accomplished in Christ Jesus our Lord. ¹²In him and through faith in him we may approach God with freedom and confidence. ¹³I ask you, therefore, not to be discouraged because of my sufferings for you, which are your glory.

The major emphasis of Ephesians 2–3 is the centrality of the body of Christ. This was God's "eternal purpose"—to create the church out of a new and reconciled humanity in union with Jesus Christ (v. 11). It was hidden in the past and then accomplished in history on the cross with results lasting into eternity. Because of this, we dare not disregard the church in the history of humanity.

Christians affirm that history is "his story," God's story. While much historical study focuses on prime ministers, presidents, politicians, and generals, the Bible concentrates on insignificant people who are at the same time God's people, a multinational community called the church, which has no territorial frontiers, which claims nothing less than the whole world for Christ, and whose empire will never come to an end.

The church is central to the gospel. The gospel some of us proclaim is much too individualistic. "Christ died for me," we say, and then sing of heaven, "Oh, that will be glory for me." Both affirmations are true. But this is far from the full gospel. The good news of the boundless riches of Christ is that he died and rose again not only to save sinners like me (though he did) but also to create a single new humanity. The gospel is good news of a new society as well as of a new life.

The church is central to Christian living, which includes both suffering and glory (v. 13). Jesus said that he would enter his glory through suffering and that his followers would have to tread the same path. Here, however, Paul writes something different, namely, that *his* sufferings will bring *them* (his Gentile readers) glory. He is suffering in prison on their behalf, as their champion, standing firm for their inclusion in God's new society. So convinced is he of the divine origin of his vision that he is prepared to pay any price to see it become a reality.

The church must surely be central to our lives. How can we take lightly what God takes so seriously? If like Paul we keep before us the vision of God's new society as his family, his dwelling place, and his instrument in the world, then we constantly will be seeking to make our church's worship more authentic, its fellowship more caring, and its outreach more compassionate.

God has not abandoned his church, however displeased with it he may be. He is still building and refining it. And if God has not abandoned it, how can we?

A Staircase of Prayer

EPHESIANS 3:14-19

[14]For this reason I kneel before the Father, [15]from whom every family in heaven and on earth derives its name. [16]I pray that out of his glorious riches he may strengthen you with power through his Spirit in your inner being, [17]so that Christ may dwell in your hearts through faith. And I pray that you, being rooted and established in love, [18]may have power, together with all the Lord's holy people, to grasp how wide and long and high and deep is the love of Christ, [19]and to know this love that surpasses knowledge—that you may be filled to the measure of all the fullness of God.

One of the best ways to discover our chief anxieties and ambitions is to reflect on the content of our prayers. Paul begins, "For this reason I kneel before the Father," resuming his train of thought where he had left it in verse 1. What moves him to pray? Surely it is both the reconciling work of Christ and his own understanding of it by special revelation.

Paul goes on to affirm that from the Father "every family in heaven and on earth derives its name." There is a deliberate play on words in the Greek sentence, since "father" is *patēr* and "family" is *patria*. Perhaps Paul is saying not only that the whole

Christian family is named from the Father, but that the very notion of fatherhood is derived from the fatherhood of God.

The apostle's petition proceeds in verses 16-19 as a staircase by which he climbs higher and higher in his aspiration for his readers in four steps. He prays first that God may *strengthen* them by the indwelling of Christ through his Spirit. Some are puzzled by this, wondering, *Surely, Christ dwells by his Spirit within every believer. Was Christ not already within them?* Indeed every Christian is indwelt by Christ and is the temple of the Holy Spirit. Nevertheless, as Charles Hodge comments, "The indwelling of Christ is a thing of degrees." Thus Paul prays to the Father that Christ by his Spirit will be allowed to settle down in their hearts, and from his throne there both control and empower them.

Second, Paul prays that they may be rooted and established in *love.* The new humanity is God's family, whose members love their Father and love each other. Or should. They need the Spirit's power and Christ's indwelling to enable them to love each other, especially across the deep racial and cultural divide that previously had separated them.

Third, he asks that they may *know* Christ's love in all its dimensions, even though it "surpasses knowledge" (vv. 18-19). Commentators warn us not to be too literal in our interpretation of these, since the apostle may only have been indulging in a little poetic hyperbole. Yet it seems to me legitimate to say that the love of Christ is wide enough to encompass all humanity, long enough to last for eternity, high enough to exalt him to heaven, and deep enough to reach the most degraded sinner.

Fourth, the apostle prays that they may be filled right up to the very *fullness* of God. Staggering as the thought may be, we are to be filled not *with* so much as *up to* the fullness of God. Such a prayer must surely look toward our final state of perfection in heaven when together we enter the completeness of God's purpose for us and are filled to capacity. Nonetheless, God expects us to grow daily as we are being transformed by the Holy Spirit into Christ's image from one degree of glory to another.

The God Who Can Answer Prayer

EPHESIANS 3:20–21

> [20]Now to him who is able to do immeasurably more than all we ask or imagine, according to his power that is at work within us, [21]to him be glory in the church and in Christ Jesus throughout all generations, for ever and ever! Amen.

As we look back down the staircase we climbed with Paul in verses 16–19, we notice now that the apostle's four petitions are sandwiched between two references to God. In verses 14–16 God is the Father of the whole family and possesses infinite riches in glory; in verses 20–21 he is the one who works powerfully within us. Such a God can answer prayer.

God's ability to answer prayer is forcefully stated by the apostle in a composite expression of seven stages. (1) He is able to *do* or to work for he is neither idle, inactive, nor dead. (2) He is able to do what *we ask*, for he hears and answers prayer. (3) He is able to do what we ask *or imagine*, for he reads our thoughts, and sometimes we dream of things for which we dare not and therefore do not ask. (4) He is able to do *all* that we ask or think, for he knows it all and can perform it all. (5) He is able to do *more than* all that we ask or think, for his expectations are higher than ours. (6) He is able to do "far more" (RSV), for he does not give his grace by calculated degree. (7) He is able to do *immeasurably* more than all that we ask or think, for he is a God of superabundance.

The infinite ability of God to work beyond our prayers, thoughts, and dreams is by the "power that is at work within us," within us individually (Christ dwelling in our hearts by faith) and within us as a people (who are the dwelling place of God by his Spirit). It is the power of the resurrection, the power that raised Christ from the dead, enthroned him in the heavenlies, and then raised and enthroned us there with him (1:19-21; 2:6). That is the power at work within Christians and the church.

Paul's prayer is about fulfilling his vision for God's new society of love. He asks that its members may be strengthened to love and to know the love of Christ though this surpasses knowledge. But then he turns from the love of God past knowing to the power of God past imagining, from limitless love to limitless power. He is convinced, as we must be, that only divine power can generate divine love in the divine society.

To add anything more would be inappropriate, except the doxology. "To him be glory," Paul exclaims, to this God of resurrection power who alone can make the dream come true. The power comes from him; the glory must go to him. To him be glory "in the church and in Christ Jesus" together, in the body and in the Head, in the bride and in the Bridegroom, in the community of peace and in the Peacemaker, "throughout all generations" (in history), "for ever and ever" (in eternity). Amen.

Ephesians 3:1-21

....

Discussion Guide

Open

What have you learned from a Christian whose background is different from yours? (Consider those who are different in terms of age, denomination, ethnicity, gender, social status, and so on.)

Study

Read Ephesians 3:1-21.

1. What do you learn about Paul in this passage?

2. Why would Paul consider himself a prisoner of Christ when in reality he was a prisoner of Nero?

3. What was this mystery that was made known to Paul through special revelation (v. 6)?

4. How are you encouraged in the ways you serve God by this description of Paul?

5. Why would God want his wisdom made known to the rulers and authorities in the heavenly realms (vv. 10-11)?

6. List all the requests in the prayer of verses 14-21.

7. Paul begins the passage, "For this reason." What was the reason for Paul's prayer?

8. How is God characterized in verses 14-15?

9. How does our understanding of God impact how we approach him in prayer?

10. As you think about all that has been explained in the book of Ephesians so far, why is love such an important element of Paul's prayer?

11. How have you seen this prayer answered in your church?

12. How is this whole prayer evidence of the freedom and confidence we can approach God with?

APPLY

1. How do you see God's grace in your daily life and ministry?

2. What is your attitude toward the church, and how might your attitude need to change?

3. How would you like to grow in the way that you pray for your church?

4. Praise God for his church, the body of Christ. Ask him to help you to grow in your appreciation of the church. Kneel quietly and in worship before the Father, from whom his whole family in heaven and earth derives its name. Pray Paul's prayer for your church.

6

Ephesians 4:1-16
Unity

[handwritten marginalia: humility is not thinking less of ...]

Unity and Love

EPHESIANS 4:1-2

[1]As a prisoner for the Lord, then, I urge you to live a life worthy of the calling you have received. [2]Be completely humble and gentle; be patient, bearing with one another in love.

For three chapters Paul has been unfolding a magnificent vision. Through Jesus Christ, God is creating something entirely new. Now the apostle moves on from the new society to the new standards expected of it. So he turns from mind-stretching theology to its down-to-earth, concrete implications in everyday living.

He implores his readers "to live a life worthy of the calling you have received." What is this? The new society God is calling into being is characterized by unity and purity. The apostle treats the unity of the church in 4:1-16 and the purity of the church in 4:17–5:21.

Paul portrays the life worthy of our calling as being characterized by five qualities—humility, gentleness, patience, mutual forbearance, and love. He tells us to be sure that we live a life of love. This is where he begins, and this is also where we should begin. Too many start with structures, but the apostle starts with moral qualities.

Humility was despised in the ancient world. The Greeks never used their word for humility in a context of approval. Instead they meant by it an abject, servile, subservient attitude. Not until Jesus Christ came was true humility recognized. He humbled himself as a servant. And only he among the world's religious and ethical teachers has set before us a little child as our model. Paul has in mind the humble recognition of the worth and value of other people.

Humility is essential to unity. When we recognize the intrinsic God-given worth of other people, we promote harmony in God's new society.

Gentleness was applauded by Aristotle because he hated extremes and loved the golden mean. The word was also used of domesticated animals, so it is not a synonym for weakness. On the contrary, it is the gentleness of the strong whose strength is under control. It is the quality of strong people who are nevertheless masters of themselves and the servants of others.

The third and fourth qualities, patience and bearing with one another, form a natural pair. Patience is longsuffering toward aggravating people, such as God in Christ showed toward us. Bearing with one another speaks of that mutual tolerance necessary for human beings to live together in peace.

Love is the final quality, which embraces the preceding four, and is the crown and sum of all virtues. To love is to seek constructively the welfare of others and the good of the community.

Here, then, are five foundation stones of Christian unity. Where these are absent, no external structure of unity can stand. But when this strong base has been laid, then there is good hope that a visible unity can be built.

Christian Unity and the Unity of Our God

EPHESIANS 4:3-6

> [3]Make every effort to keep the unity of the Spirit through the bond of peace. [4]There is one body and one Spirit, just as you were called to one hope when you were called; [5]one Lord, one faith, one baptism; [6]one God and Father of all, who is over all and through all and in all.

Even the casual reader of verses 3-6 is struck by Paul's repetition of the word *one*. In fact, it occurs seven times, three referencing the three persons of the Trinity, and the other four alluding to our Christian experience in relation to the three persons of the Trinity.

There is one body because there is only one Spirit (v. 4). The one body is the church, the body of Christ (1:23), comprising Jewish and Gentile believers; and its unity or cohesion is due to the one Holy Spirit.

There is one hope belonging to our Christian calling (v. 4), one faith, and one baptism (v. 5) because there is only one Lord. It is Jesus Christ we have believed in, Jesus Christ we have been baptized into, and Jesus Christ who we wait for with expectant hope.

There is one Christian family, embracing us all (v. 6) because "one God and Father of all, who is over all and through all and in all."

We must assert that there *can* be only one Christian family; only one Christian faith, hope, and baptism; and only one Christian body, because there is only one God—Father, Son, and Holy Spirit. How, then, can the disunity of the church be reconciled with the biblical insistence on the indestructibility of its unity?

The apostle himself recognizes this paradoxical combination of unity and disunity. For in this very passage, in which the indestructible unity of the church is so emphatically asserted, the possibility of disunity is also acknowledged. Consider verse 3: we are told to "make every effort to keep the unity of the Spirit through the bond of peace." What does Paul mean? To maintain the church's unity must mean to maintain it visibly. We are to demonstrate to the world that the unity we say exists indestructibly is not the rather sick joke it sounds but a true and glorious reality.

Consider a human family—husband, wife, and three sons. Over time the father and mother quarrel, keep up an uneasy truce, but finally get a divorce. The three boys also argue, first with their parents and then with each other. They never meet, text, or call. Now suppose we are cousins of this family, how would we react? Would we shrug our shoulders and mutter, "Oh, well, never mind, they are still one family, you know"? No, this would not satisfy either our minds or our hearts. Surely we would seek to be peacemakers.

Just so, the fact of the church's indestructible unity is no excuse for acquiescing in the tragedy of its actual disunity. Some Christian fellowships are marred by rivalries between individuals or groups that have festered for years. How can we possibly condone such things? We need to be eager for love, unity, and peace. We need to actively seek it.

Serving Grace

EPHESIANS 4:7-10

> [7] But to each one of us grace has been given as Christ apportioned it. [8] This is why it says:

> "When he ascended on high,
>   he took many captives
>   and gave gifts to his people."

> [9] (What does "he ascended" mean except that he also descended to the lower, earthly regions? [10] He who descended is the very one who ascended higher than all the heavens, in order to fill the whole universe.)

The contrast between verses 6 and 7 is striking. Paul turns from the Father of *all of us* to the gifts given *each of us*, from the unity to the diversity of the church. He is, in fact, deliberately qualifying what he has just written about the church's unity. Although there is only one body, one faith, and one family, this unity is not to be misconstrued as a lifeless or colorless uniformity. On the contrary, the unity of the church is exciting in its diversity.

What does he tell us about these gifts? *Saving grace* is given to all sinners who believe. But in verse 7 Paul speaks of what might be termed *service grace*, the grace that equips God's people for ministry. We get the word *charismatic* from the Greek word *charismata*. Some groups deliberately take the term *charismatic* to describe themselves, but according to the New Testament the whole church is a charismatic community. Every single member has a gift (*charisma*) to exercise or function to perform.

In verse 8 Paul says more about spiritual gifts by quoting from Psalm 68:18. The psalm is a call to God to come to the rescue of his people and vindicate them again, as in olden days. After every conquest in the ancient world, tribute was received and gifts distributed. What conquerors took from their captives, they gave away to their own people. The spoils were divided; the booty was shared.

Paul applies this picture to Christ's ascension. He ascended as conqueror to the Father's right hand, his train of captives being the principalities and powers he had defeated, dethroned, and disarmed.

After the quotation from Psalm 68:18 Paul adds in parenthesis that the ascension of Christ implies that "he also descended to the lower, earthly regions" (v. 9). The early fathers understood this as a reference to his descent into Hades as suggested in 1 Peter 3:19. Calvin argued that Christ's descent refers to his incarnation. The NIV seems to take it this way too, namely, that he descended from heaven "to the lower, earthly regions." Perhaps, however, the reference is more general still, namely, that Christ descended to the depths of humiliation when he came to earth.

In the light of this emphasis on Christ ascended, exalted, filling the universe, ruling the church, and bestowing gifts, it would clearly be a mistake to think of *charismata* as being exclusively gifts of the Spirit and to associate them too closely with the Holy Spirit or with experiences of the Holy Spirit. For here they are the gifts of Christ, while in Romans 12 they are the gifts of God the Father. It is always misleading to separate the three persons of the Trinity. Together they are involved in every aspect of the church's well-being.

The Variety of Gifts

EPHESIANS 4:11

> [11]So Christ himself gave the apostles, the prophets, the evangelists, the pastors and teachers.

The word *apostle* has three main meanings in the New Testament. Only once it seems to be applied to every individual Christian, when Jesus said that a messenger (*apostolos*) is not "greater than the one who sent him" (John 13:16). So every Christian is both a servant and an apostle. Second, there were apostles of the churches (2 Corinthians 8:23), messengers sent out by a church either as missionaries or on some other errand. And third, there were the apostles of Christ, consisting of the Twelve, Paul, James the Lord's brother, and possibly one or two others chosen and authorized by Jesus.

It seems Paul is using the word here in this last sense, for this is how he has used the word in his letter, referring to himself (1:1) and to his fellow apostles as the foundation of the church

(2:20; 3:5). In this sense there are no apostles today. We can nonetheless argue for those with apostolic ministries of a different kind, including episcopal jurisdiction, pioneer missionary work, church planting, itinerant leadership, and so forth.

What about *prophets*? A prophet was a mouthpiece of God, a vehicle of his direct revelation. In this sense we must again insist that there are no prophets today. Nobody can presume to claim an inspiration comparable to the canonical prophets or a legitimate use of their introductory formula "Thus says the Lord."

But some see the gift of prophecy as a special gift of biblical preaching, though not as new revelation. Others see it as a deep perception of the contemporary world, a reading of the signs of the times, together with an indignant denunciation of the social sins like the sociopolitical oracles of the Old Testament prophets. A third view concentrates on the effect the ministry of New Testament prophets had on their listeners, bringing conviction of sin to unbelievers, and encouragement and comfort to believers. In all three views the prophetic gift is detected in the handling of the Word of God.

After apostles and prophets Paul mentions evangelists. Since all Christians are under obligation to bear witness to Christ and his good news, the gift of an evangelist (bestowed only on some) must be something different. It may refer to the gift of evangelistic preaching or of making the gospel particularly plain and relevant to unbelievers, or of effective personal witness.

Since the definite article is not repeated regarding pastors and teachers, it may be that these are two names for the same ministry. Pastors (that is, shepherds), who are called to tend

God's flock, do so in particular by feeding it, that is, by teaching. Although all pastors must be teachers, perhaps not all Christian teachers are also pastors since they may be teaching in a school or college rather than in a local church.

All five gifts relate in some way to the ministry of teaching. Nothing is more necessary for the building up of God's church in every age than an ample supply of God-gifted teachers.

Equipping for Service

EPHESIANS 4:12

[12]to equip his people for works of service, so that the body of Christ may be built up.

Paul offers two reasons why Christ gave these gifts to his church—one immediate and the other ultimate. The word *service* (*diakonia*) is here used not to describe the work of pastors but rather the work of all God's people without exception. The New Testament envisions ministry not as the prerogative of a clerical elite but as the privileged calling of all the people of God.

There is still a distinctive pastoral ministry left for clergy, but clearly it is not of people who jealously guard all ministry in their own hands, successfully squashing all lay initiatives. Rather it is of those who help and encourage all God's people to discover, develop, and exercise their gifts. Instead of monopolizing all ministry, they multiply it.

What model of the church, then, should we keep in our minds? The traditional model is that of the pyramid, with the pastor perched precariously on its pinnacle, like a little pope in his own church, while the laity are arrayed beneath him in ranks of inferiority. It is an unbiblical image, because the New Testament envisions not a single pastor with a docile flock but both a plural oversight and an every-member ministry. The church is the body of Christ, every member of which has a distinctive function. There is simply no room either for a hierarchy or a bossy clericalism.

I saw the principle of the every-member ministry well illustrated when I visited St. Paul's Church in Darien, Connecticut. On the front cover of their Sunday bulletin I read the name of the rector, then the names of the associate rector, and of the assistant to the rector. Next came the following line: "Ministers: the entire congregation." It was startling but undeniably biblical.

So Christ's immediate purpose in giving pastors and teachers to his church is so that through their ministry of the Word all his people are equipped for their varied ministries. The ultimate purpose of this is to build up the church. These gifts are so beneficial both to those who exercise their ministry faithfully and to those who receive it that the church becomes steadily more healthy and mature.

All spiritual gifts, then, are service gifts. They are not given for selfish but for unselfish use, namely, to serve other people "for the common good" (1 Corinthians 12:7). While some gifts are greater than others (1 Corinthians 12:31), we determine this by the degree to which they build up the church. This is why the teaching gifts are of paramount importance, for nothing builds up the church like the truth of God's Word.

The exalted Christ bestows gifts on his church, gifts that are very diverse, their purpose being to equip God's people for their ministries and so build up Christ's body.

Unity in Maturity

EPHESIANS 4:13-16

> [13]until we all reach unity in the faith and in the knowledge of the Son of God and become mature, attaining to the whole measure of the fullness of Christ.
> [14]Then we will no longer be infants, tossed back and forth by the waves, and blown here and there by every wind of teaching and by the cunning and craftiness of people in their deceitful scheming. [15]Instead, speaking the truth in love, we will grow to become in every respect the mature body of him who is the head, that is, Christ. [16]From him the whole body, joined and held together by every supporting ligament, grows and builds itself up in love, as each part does its work.

The apostle elaborates what he means by building up the body of Christ. Just as unity needs to be maintained *visibly*, so it needs to be attained *fully*. The unity we are to come to one day is that full unity that a full faith in and knowledge of the Son of God will make possible (v. 13).

This full unity is mature, and the context seems to demand that we understand it corporately. The church is represented as a single organism, the body of Christ, and is to grow up into adult stature. Indeed, Paul has referred to it as "one new

humanity" (2:15). To the oneness and the newness he now adds
"matureness," which will be nothing less than "the whole measure
of the fullness of Christ."

Although this growth into maturity is a corporate concept,
describing the church as a whole, it clearly depends on the ma-
turing of its individual members since Paul expects that "then
we will no longer be infants" (v. 14). Of course we are to resemble
children in their humility and innocence, but not in their ignorance or instability.

Unstable children are like little boats in a stormy sea, entirely
at the mercy of wind and waves. Such are immature Christians.
They never seem to know their own mind or come to settled
convictions. Instead, they fall an easy prey to each new theological fad. They cannot resist "the cunning and craftiness of
people in their deceitful scheming." In contrast, we should be
"speaking the truth in love" so that "we will grow to become in
every respect the mature body of him who is the head, that is,
Christ" (v. 15).

However, "speaking the truth in love" is not the best ren-
dering of his expression, for the Greek verb makes no reference
to our speech. Literally, it means, "truthing in love," and includes
the notions of maintaining, living, and doing the truth.

There are those in the contemporary church who are determined at all costs to defend and uphold God's revealed truth.
But sometimes they are conspicuously lacking in love. When
they think they smell heresy, their nose begins to twitch, their
muscles ripple, and the light of battle enters their eye. They seem
to enjoy nothing more than a fight. Others make the opposite

mistake. They are determined at all costs to maintain and exhibit love, but in order to do so are prepared even to sacrifice the central truths of revelation.

Both these tendencies are unbalanced and unbiblical. Truth becomes hard if it is not softened by love; love becomes soft if it is not strengthened by truth. The apostle calls us to hold the two together, which should not be difficult for Spirit-filled believers, since the Holy Spirit is himself the Spirit of truth and his first fruit is love. There is no other route than this to a fully mature Christian unity.

Ephesians 4:1-16

....

Discussion Guide

Open

How is unity different from uniformity?

Study

Read Ephesians 4:1-16.

1. What does Paul urge the Ephesians to do in verses 1-6?

2. Because God's people are called to be one people, they must manifest their unity. Define each of the characteristics (humbleness, gentleness, patience, forbearance, love) to which Paul calls them in verse 2.

3. How would following the instructions in verse 2 contribute to the unity of the church?

4. In what kinds of situations do you struggle with the tension between humility and pride?

5. In verses 4-6 Paul repeats the word *one* seven times, and three of those allude to the persons of the Trinity. How does unity of our God relate to Christian unity?

6. Why would Paul need to urge the Ephesian believers to make every effort to keep the unity just before making such a strong statement about the body being one in verse 4?

7. How does Paul make it clear that unity does not mean uniformity?

8. What do we learn about the giver of spiritual gifts in verses 9-10?

9. What do we learn about the purpose of spiritual gifts (vv. 12-16)?

10. What does Paul mean by building up the body of Christ, according to verses 13-16?

11. The church grows by truth and love. Give some examples of what happens when we minimize one or the other.

APPLY

1. Which of the qualities of unity discussed in this passage have helped you experience unity with others?

2. What have you done to maintain and work for the unity of the Spirit in your Christian community?

3. How would you like to grow in the ways you use your spiritual gifts to fulfill the purposes listed in verses 11-13? (This could include thinking of ways to become more familiar with your gifts.)

4. Thank God for the marvelous unity that he has made available to us in the church. Confess to him the ways that

you have failed to strive to maintain unity in your church. Ask him to change you and build into you the five foundation stones of Christian unity.

7

Ephesians 4:17–5:4
Purity

❧

The Darkened Mind

EPHESIANS 4:17-19

¹⁷So I tell you this, and insist on it in the Lord, that you must no longer live as the Gentiles do, in the futility of their thinking. ¹⁸They are darkened in their understanding and separated from the life of God because of the ignorance that is in them due to the hardening of their hearts. ¹⁹ Having lost all sensitivity, they have given themselves over to sensuality so as to indulge in every kind of impurity, and they are full of greed.

Paul continues to describe the new standards expected of God's new society, or the life worthy of God's call. Called to be one people, we must cultivate unity. Called to be a holy people, we must also cultivate purity.

The gist of his message is plain: "you must no longer live as the Gentiles do." He is generalizing of course. Not all pagans were (or are) as dissolute as those he is about to portray. Yet just as there is a typical Christian life, so there is a typical pagan life. His readers knew from experience what he was saying; for they had been pagans themselves, and they were still living in a pagan environment. But they must live that way no longer, even if those around them continued to do so. Once they were pagans and lived like pagans; now they were Christians and must live like Christians.

It was essential at the outset for his readers to grasp the contrast between what they had been as pagans and what they now were as Christians, and further to grasp the underlying theological basis of this change. While describing pagans, he draws attention to the futility of their thinking, adding that they are darkened in their understanding while attributing their alienation from God to the ignorance that is in them. As a result they had become callous, licentious, and insatiably unclean.

But what is the origin of the darkness of heathen minds? It is "due to the hardening of their hearts" (v. 18). NEB translates it "their minds have grown hard as stone" while the GNT uses "stubborn." It is true that in biblical usage heart and mind cannot be separated, since the heart includes our capacity to think and understand. Nevertheless, there is a real distinction between ignorance on the one hand and hardness or obstinacy on the other.

If we put Paul's expressions together, noting carefully their logical connections, he seems to be depicting the terrible downward path of evil, which begins with an obstinate rejection of God's known truth. Hardness of heart leads first to darkness of mind, then to deadness of soul under the judgment of God, and finally to recklessness of life. NEB has, "They stop at nothing to satisfy their foul desire." Thus having lost all sensitivity, people lose all self-control.

In verses 20-24 we will see that over against the darkness and ignorance of the heathen Paul sets the truth of Christ that Christians had learned. Scripture bears an unwavering testimony to the power of ignorance and error to corrupt, and the power of truth to liberate, ennoble, and refine.

The Christian Life

EPHESIANS 4:20-24

> [20]That, however, is not the way of life you learned [21]when you heard about Christ and were taught in him in accordance with the truth that is in Jesus. [22]You were taught, with regard to your former way of life, to put off your old self, which is being corrupted by its deceitful desires; [23]to be made new in the attitude of your minds; [24]and to put on the new self, created to be like God in true righteousness and holiness.

Over against heathen hardness, darkness, and recklessness Paul sets a whole process of Christian moral education. He uses three parallel expressions: *you learned* (v. 20), *you heard* (v. 21), and *you were taught* (v. 21).

According to the first, Christ is himself the substance of Christian teaching. He is the Word made flesh, the unique God-man, who died, rose, and reigns. But more than that, we must also preach his lordship, the kingdom or rule of righteousness he ushered in, and all the moral demands of the new life. The Christ the Ephesians had learned was calling them to standards and values totally at variance with their former pagan life.

Second, we have Christ the teacher (you heard him). It is a pity that NIV translates the phrase "you heard about Christ," for there is no preposition. Paul assumes that through the voice of their Christian teachers, they had actually heard Christ's voice. Thus, when sound biblical moral instruction is being given, it may be said that Christ is teaching about Christ.

Third, they had been taught in him. That is, Jesus Christ was also the context, even the atmosphere within which the teaching was given. When Jesus Christ is at once the subject, the object, and the environment of the moral instruction being given, we may have confidence that it is truly Christian. For "truth . . . is in Jesus." But what exactly is this truth in Jesus? If heathen darkness leads to reckless uncleanness, verses 22–24 give the answer. It is nothing less than putting off our old humanity like a rotten garment and putting on like clean clothing the new humanity re-created in God's image.

Paul's readers had been taught that becoming a Christian involves a radical change, namely, conversion and re-creation. It involves the repudiation of our former self, our fallen humanity, and the assumption of a new self or re-created humanity.

The portraits Paul paints of both selves balance one another. The old was in the process of degenerating, on its way to ruin or destruction; the new has been freshly "created to be like God."

The new humanity we assume is God's creation, not ours, but we entirely concur with what he has done. We "put off" our old life, turning away from it in distaste, and we "put on" the new life he has created, embracing it and welcoming it with joy. In a word, re-creation (what God does) and repentance (what we do by his grace) belong together and cannot be separated.

The kind of clothing we wear depends on the kind of role we are fulfilling. But when we change our role, we change our dress. Since by a new creation we have put off the old humanity and put on the new, we must also put away the old standards and adopt new ones. Our new role will mean new clothing, our new life a new ethical lifestyle.

What Breaks Fellowship

EPHESIANS 4:25-27

> [25]Therefore each of you must put off falsehood and speak
> truthfully to your neighbor, for we are all members of one
> body. [26]"In your anger do not sin": Do not let the sun go
> down while you are still angry, [27]and do not give the devil
> a foothold.

It is marvelous how Paul can easily descend from lofty theological talk about our two humanities to the nitty-gritty of Christian behavior.

He begins with lies and truth. Strictly speaking, the Greek word is not *falsehood* in the abstract but "the lie." So it is possible, therefore, that Paul is referring here to the great lie of idolatry, the chief symptom of a futile and darkened mind (4:17-18). He urges them now to forsake all lesser lies and speak the truth.

The followers of Jesus should be known in their community as honest, reliable people whose word can be trusted. The reason given is not only that the other person is our *neighbor*, whom we are commanded in Scripture to love, but Paul brings us back to his doctrine of the church: "for we are all members of one body" (vv. 12-16). Fellowship is built on trust, and trust is built on truth. So falsehood undermines fellowship, while truth strengthens it.

Next Paul urges, "In your anger do not sin," an echo of Psalm 4:4. The NIV correctly renders this Hebrew idiom that permits and then restricts anger. Scripture plainly teaches that there are two kinds of anger, righteous and unrighteous. In 4:31 anger is one of a number of unpleasant things we are to put away. But in 5:6 we are told of the anger of God that will fall on the disobedient, and we know that God's anger is righteous. So was the anger of Jesus (Mark 3:5).

We greatly need more Christian anger today. In the face of blatant evil we should be indignant, not tolerant; angry, not apathetic. If God hates sin, his people should hate it too. Paul knows that true peace is not identical with appeasement.

At the same time, we always have to be on our guard and act as censors of our own anger. So Paul immediately qualifies his permissive *be angry* by three negatives.

First, "do not sin." We have to make sure that our anger is free from injured pride, spite, malice, animosity, and the spirit of revenge. Second, "do not let the sun go down while you are still angry." Paul doesn't mean we have the freedom to be angry until sunset. No, his intention is to warn us against nursing anger. It is seldom safe to allow the embers to smolder. "Never go to bed angry" is a good rule of thumb, and is seldom more applicable than to a married couple. Paul's third qualification is "do not give the devil a foothold," for he knows how fine is the line between righteous and unrighteous anger, and how hard human beings find it to handle their anger responsibly.

In every case, we must be vigilant not to provoke a breach of fellowship.

Using Our Hands and Mouths

EPHESIANS 4:28-30

[28]Anyone who has been stealing must steal no longer, but must work, doing something useful with their own hands, that they may have something to share with those in need.

[29]Do not let any unwholesome talk come out of your mouths, but only what is helpful for building others up according to their needs, that it may benefit those who listen. [30]And do not grieve the Holy Spirit of God, with whom you were sealed for the day of redemption.

Paul's practical advice continues with a reference to the eighth commandment: do not steal. It has a wide application, not only to the stealing of other people's money or possessions, but also to tax evasions and customs dodges that rob the government of its dues, to employers who do not pay fair wages, and to employees who give poor service or work short time.

In echoing the commandment, however, the apostle goes beyond the prohibition and draws out its positive implications. It is not enough to stop stealing. We should start working, honest, useful work so we can earn our own living, be able to support our family, and be able to give to "those in need."

The apostle then turns from the use of our hands to the use of our mouths. Speech is a wonderful gift of God. So "do not let any unwholesome talk come out of your mouths." Paul uses a word here for rotten trees and rotten fruit. Instead, we are to use our unique gift of speech constructively, to build people up and not damage or destroy them.

Instead of hurting people with our words, we want to use them to help, encourage, cheer, comfort, and stimulate them. I have myself often been challenged by the contrasting speech of the wise man and the fool in Proverbs 12:18: "The words of the reckless pierce like swords, but the tongue of the wise brings healing."

Paul then introduces the Holy Spirit, "Do not grieve the Holy Spirit of God, with whom you were sealed for the day of redemption" (v. 30), perhaps because he was constantly aware that invisible personalities are present and active (v. 27). But what grieves him? Since he is the "Holy Spirit," he is always grieved by unholiness, and since he is the "one Spirit" (2:18; 4:4), disunity will also cause him grief. In fact, anything incompatible with the purity or unity of the church is incompatible with his own nature and therefore hurts him.

We notice also in verse 30 the references to being "sealed" with the Spirit and to "the day of redemption." The sealing took place at the beginning of our Christian life (1:13); the Holy Spirit himself, indwelling us, is the seal with which God has stamped us as his own. Although we already have redemption in the sense of forgiveness (1:7), the day of redemption looks forward to the end when our bodies will be redeemed, for only then will our redemption or liberation be complete.

So the sealing and the redemption refer respectively to the beginning and the end of the salvation process. And in between these two termini we are to grow in Christlikeness and take care not to grieve the Holy Spirit. Every Spirit-filled believer desires to bring him pleasure.

Copy God

EPHESIANS 4:31–5:2

> [31]Get rid of all bitterness, rage and anger, brawling and slander, along with every form of malice. [32]Be kind and compassionate to one another, forgiving each other, just as in Christ God forgave you. [5:1]Follow God's example, therefore, as dearly loved children [2]and walk in the way of love, just as Christ loved us and gave himself up for us as a fragrant offering and sacrifice to God.

Paul now offers a series of six unpleasant attitudes and actions we are to put away entirely. "Bitterness" is a sour spirit and sour speech. We sometimes talk about a sourpuss, and I guess there are sour tomcats too. Little is sadder in elderly people than a negative and cynical outlook on life.

"Rage and anger" are obviously similar, the former denoting a passionate outburst and the latter a more settled and sullen hostility. "Brawling" describes people who get excited, raise their voices in a quarrel, and start shouting, even screaming, at each other, while "slander" is speaking evil of others, especially behind their backs, and so defaming and even destroying their reputation. The sixth word is "malice," or ill will, wishing and probably plotting evil against people. Alternatively, it may be inclusive of the five preceding vices. There is no place for any of these horrid things in the Christian community; they have to be totally rejected.

In their place we should welcome the kind of qualities that characterize the behavior of God and his Christ. We are to be kind to one another. The word is *chrēstos*, and because of the obvious assonance with the name of Christ (*Christos*), Christians from the beginning saw its peculiar appropriateness. It occurs in the Sermon on the Mount for God's kindness toward even "the ungrateful and wicked" (Luke 6:35). Further, we are to be compassionate while forgiving one another (literally "acting in grace" toward one another) as God in Christ has acted in grace toward us.

"Therefore," because of God's gracious attitude and generous actions toward us, we are to "follow God's example . . . as dearly loved children." Just as children copy their parents, so we are to copy our Father God, as Jesus told us to (Matthew 5:45, 48). We are to do this by walking "in the way of love, just as Christ loved us and gave himself up for us." The same verb for self-giving is used of the heathen in 4:19. They give themselves up to licentiousness; we, like Christ, are to give ourselves up to love. Such self-giving for others is pleasing to God. As with Christ so with us, self-sacrificial love is "a fragrant offering and sacrifice to God." It is thus a striking truth that sacrificial love for others becomes a sacrifice acceptable to God.

We can't help but notice how God-centered Paul's ethic is. It is natural for him, in issuing his moral instructions, to mention the three persons of the Trinity, telling us to copy God, to learn Christ, and not to grieve the Holy Spirit.

Giving Thanks for, Not Demeaning, God's Gift

EPHESIANS 5:3-4

> [3]But among you there must not be even a hint of sexual immorality, or of any kind of impurity, or of greed, because these are improper for God's holy people. [4]Nor should there be obscenity, foolish talk or coarse joking, which are out of place, but rather thanksgiving.

Paul's language covers every kind of sexual sin, in other words all sexual activity outside its God-ordained context of a loving marriage. Paul adds "greed," surely because it is an especially degrading form of immorality, namely, the coveting of somebody else's body for selfish gratification. The tenth commandment had specifically prohibited coveting a neighbor's wife, and earlier in this letter Paul has written of the greed involved in unclean practices (4:19). We are not only to avoid their indulgence, but also to avoid thinking and talking about them, so completely are they to be banished from the Christian community.

This was a high and holy standard to demand, for immorality was rife in that part of the Roman Empire. And since the Greek goddess Artemis, "Diana of the Ephesians," was regarded as a fertility goddess, sexual orgies were regularly associated with her worship.

Verse 4 goes beyond immorality to vulgarity. For "obscenity, foolish talk or coarse joking" are the cheapest form of wit. All three refer to a dirty mind expressing itself in dirty conversation. But these things are completely "out of place." Instead, let there be thanksgiving. The contrast is striking and beautiful. In itself thanksgiving is not an obvious substitute for vulgarity, since the latter is essentially self-centered, and the former God-centered. But perhaps this is the point that Paul is making.

Many think Christianity has a compulsively prudish attitude toward sex. And it is true that some of our Victorian forebears came close to this identification. But the reason why Christians should dislike and avoid vulgarity is not because we have a warped view of sex, and are either ashamed or afraid of it, but because we have a high and holy view of it as being in its right place God's good gift. All God's gifts, including sex, are subjects for thanksgiving, rather than for joking. To joke about them is bound to degrade them; to thank God for them is the way to preserve their worth as the blessings of a loving Creator.

Chapters 4–5 are a stirring summons to the unity and purity of the church, but they are more than that. Their theme is the integration of Christian experience (what we are), Christian theology (what we believe), and Christian ethics (how we behave). They emphasize that being, thought, and action belong together and must never be separated. For what we are governs how we think, and how we think determines how we act. We are God's new society, a people who have put off the old life and put on the new; that is what he has made us.

Ephesians 4:17–5:4

....

Discussion Guide

Open

On a scale from 1-10, 10 being most pure in its behavior and 1 the least, how would you rate the church today? Explain.

Study

Read Ephesians 4:17–5:4.

1. Paul insists that the Ephesian Christians must no longer live like pagans (Gentiles). How are the pagans described (vv. 17-19)?

2. Looking at verses 20-24 describe the process of moral education that the Christians experienced.

3. What is the role of the mind in the behavior of both the pagans (v. 18) and the believers (vv. 20-24)?

4. Why is the mind (what we are taught and what we think) so critical in matters of behavior?

5. How can we renew our minds in Christ?

6. List the sins that we are to put off, noting the positive command with each instruction (vv. 29-31).

7. What do all of these have in common?

8. What reason is given or implied in each case for the commands?

9. Why does Paul introduce the Holy Spirit in verse 30?

10. In verse 25 Paul states, "For we are all members of one body." What would be the effects of obeying these commands on the body of Christ?

APPLY

1. To which of these areas of sin that we are to put off are you vulnerable?

2. How does our identity in Christ affect the way you want to live?

3. Holiness is not a mystical condition experienced in relation to God, in isolation from human beings. We cannot be good in a vacuum but only in the real world of people. How can others help us to become more pure in behavior?

4. Thank God for his call to a life of holiness. Ask him to reveal to you sin that needs to be put off and the good garments that he wants you to put on. Thank him for the work of the Holy Spirit in your life.

8

Ephesians 5:5-21
Righteousness

❦

Idolatry and the Kingdom

EPHESIANS 5:5

⁵For of this you can be sure: No immoral, impure or greedy
person—such a person is an idolater—has any inheritance
in the kingdom of Christ and of God.

Although verse 5 continues the topic of sex, we become aware
that the emphasis has changed. Paul moves on in his treatment
of Christian behavior from models to motivation, and adds
powerful incentives to righteous living.

All employers in business and industry know the vital importance of incentives. How can workers be persuaded to work
harder and better, and so increase productivity or sales? All kinds
of inducement are offered in the form of higher wages, more
attractive conditions, bonuses, holidays, recreational and educa-
tional facilities, and then retirement and pension prospects. The
best incentives are neither material nor selfish, however. Wise

employers seek to give their workforce a heightened interest in their job, a greater loyalty to the firm, and a feeling of pride in what they are making or selling. All this bears witness to the nature of humans, made in God's likeness, who in addition to a job need reasons for doing it, ideals to inspire them, and a sense of creative fulfillment. Not surprisingly, therefore, the Bible is itself concerned not only with obligation but with motivation. People know what they ought to do; how can they be motivated to do it? Here, an aspect of the doctrine of sanctification (the process of becoming like Christ), is emphasized.

The first incentive Paul mentions is the solemn certainty of judgment. Most immoral people get away with their immorality on earth, but they will not escape detection, conviction, and sentence forever. "For this you can be sure," Paul warns, "no immoral, impure or greedy person . . . has any inheritance in the kingdom of Christ and of God." The immoral or impure people envisioned here are those who have given themselves up to this way of life without shame or penitence. This is someone who is sexually greedy (4:19; 5:3), that is, Paul adds in parenthesis, an idolater. Such people, whose lust has become an idolatrous obsession, will have no share in the perfect kingdom of God.

We must be cautious, however, in our application of this severe statement. It should not be understood as teaching that even a single immoral thought, word, or deed is enough to disqualify us from heaven; otherwise, which of us would ever qualify for admission? No. For those who fall into such sins through weakness, but afterwards repent in shame and humility, there is forgiveness.

The Certainty of Judgment

EPHESIANS 5:6-7

> ⁶ Let no one deceive you with empty words, for because of such things God's wrath comes on those who are disobedient. ⁷ Therefore do not be partners with them.

The apostle has himself urged his readers to acknowledge the truth of divine judgment. Now he warns them of the "empty words" of false teachers who would persuade them otherwise. In Paul's day Gnostics were arguing that bodily sins could be committed without damage to the soul, and with impunity. In our day there are many such deceivers in the world, and even in the church. They teach that God is too kind to condemn everybody, and that everybody will get to heaven in the end, irrespective of their behavior on earth. But their words are empty and their teaching deceitful. Universalism (that is, universal final salvation) is a lie. The truth is that "because of such things" (these evil, immoral, greedy, idolatrous practices) "God's wrath comes on those who are disobedient." The last phrase is a Hebraism already encountered in 2:2; it means those who know God's law and willfully disobey it. God's wrath falls on such, beginning now and culminating in the day of judgment.

"Therefore," Paul concludes, because God's kingdom is righteous and God's wrath will overtake the unrighteous, "do not be partners with them." Paul is not prohibiting all contact or association with such people. Otherwise we could not bring them the good news or seek to restrain them from their evil ways. And we would need to go out of the world altogether, which Christ has forbidden (John 17:15). The Greek word refers to participation, not just association. For if we share in their practices, as Lot was warned in Sodom, we run the risk of sharing in their doom.

It would be easy for Christians to speed read a paragraph like this, without pausing for reflection, on the assumption that it applies to unbelievers, not to us. Has not Paul assured us in the earlier part of his letter of our heavenly inheritance, taught us that the Holy Spirit within us is God's guarantee, even foretaste and first installment, of it until we possess it, and prayed that our eyes might be opened to see "the riches of his glorious inheritance" that will one day be ours (1:13-14, 18)? Yes, indeed he has. At the same time he also addresses to us this warning about the danger of forfeiting our inheritance in God's kingdom. How can we reconcile these things? Only by recalling that assurance of salvation is neither a synonym nor an excuse for presumption. And if we should fall into a life of greedy immorality, we would be supplying clear evidence that we are after all idolaters, not worshipers of God, disobedient people instead of obedient, and so the heirs not of heaven but of hell. The apostle gives us a solemn warning; we are wise to heed it.

The Fruit of Light

EPHESIANS 5:8-14

[8]For you were once darkness, but now you are light in the Lord. Live as children of light [9](for the fruit of the light consists in all goodness, righteousness and truth) [10]and

find out what pleases the Lord. [11]Have nothing to do with the fruitless deeds of darkness, but rather expose them. [12]It is shameful even to mention what the disobedient do in secret. [13]But everything exposed by the light becomes visible—and everything that is illuminated becomes a light. [14]This is why it is said:

> "Wake up, sleeper,
>> rise from the dead,
>> and Christ will shine on you."

Paul gives an additional reason for not getting involved in the evil conduct of immoral people. The whole paragraph plays on the rich symbolism of darkness and light, with darkness representing ignorance, error, and evil, while light represents truth and righteousness. Notice that he does not say they used to be *in* darkness but now were *in* the light. This would have been true, but what Paul writes here is more striking still: they themselves *had been* darkness and now actually *are* light. This radical transformation had taken place "in the Lord," by virtue of their union with him who claimed to be the light of the world. Consequently they must "live as children of light" or "like people who belong to the light" (GNT). Their behavior must conform to their new identity.

In practice this will mean a life shining with "all goodness, righteousness and truth" for these things are "the fruit of the light." The light metaphor speaks vividly of Christian openness and transparency, of living joyfully in the presence of Christ, with nothing to hide or fear.

Verse 13 elaborates the double value of a Christian exposure of evil. First, "everything exposed by the light becomes visible." Evil is seen for what it is without any possibility of concealment or subterfuge.

Second, "everything that is illuminated becomes a light." Paul seems to be describing a second stage in what light does: it actually transforms what it illumines into light. This may mean that Christians who lead a righteous life thereby restrain and reform evildoers, yes, and even convert them. The light that exposes has positive evangelistic power also. It may bring people, as they see the ugliness of evil, to conviction of their sin and so to penitent faith in Jesus.

Verse 14 is a natural conclusion. Paul clinches his argument with an apt quotation, which either summarizes the teaching of an Old Testament verse like Isaiah 61:1 or, as many modern commentators suggest, is an extract from an Easter or baptismal hymn: "Wake up, sleeper, rise from the dead, and Christ will shine on you." Here our former condition in Adam is graphically described in terms of sleep, death, and darkness, which Christ rescues us from. Conversion is nothing less than awaking out of sleep, rising from death, and being brought out of darkness into the light of Christ. No wonder we are summoned to live a new life in consequence!

The Nature of Wisdom

EPHESIANS 5:15-17

> [15]Be very careful, then, how you live—not as unwise but as wise, [16]making the most of every opportunity, because the

days are evil. [17] Therefore do not be foolish, but understand what the Lord's will is.

Everything worth doing requires care. We all take trouble over the things that seem to us to matter—our job, our education, our home and family, our hobbies, our dress and appearance. So as Christians, Paul says, we must take trouble over our Christian life. We must treat it as the serious thing it is. What, therefore, are the marks of wise people who take trouble over their Christian discipleship?

First, wise people make the most of every opportunity. The Greek verb probably means "to buy up," to get the most out of every chance we have to do good. Certainly wise people know that time is a precious commodity. All of us have the same amount of time at our disposal. None of us can stretch time. But wise people use it to the fullest possible advantage. They know that time is passing and also that "the days are evil." So they seize each fleeting opportunity while it is there. For once it has passed, even the wisest people cannot recover it.

Second, wise people discern the will of God. They are sure that wisdom is to be found in God's will and nowhere else. Jesus himself prayed, "Not my will but yours be done," and taught us to pray, "May your will be done on earth as in heaven." Nothing is more important in life than to discover and do the will of God.

In seeking to discover God's will, we must distinguish between his general and his particular will. His general will relates to all of us—that is, to become like Christ. His particular will, however, concerns the specifics of our life, and is different for each of us—what career we will follow, whether we should marry, and if so, whom. We find his general will in Scripture. We do not find his particular will there. To be sure, we find general principles in Scripture to guide us, but detailed decisions have to be made after careful thought and prayer, and the seeking of advice from mature and experienced believers.

The Fullness of the Holy Spirit

EPHESIANS 5:18

> [18]Do not get drunk on wine, which leads to debauchery. Instead, be filled with the Spirit.

The Christian duty and privilege is the command, "Be filled with the Spirit." Paul has already told his readers that they have been sealed with and must not grieve the Holy Spirit (1:13; 4:30). Now he offers no greater secret of holiness than to be filled by the One whose very nature and name are holy.

When Paul says, "Be filled with the Spirit," this is not a tentative proposal but an authoritative command. To be filled with the Spirit is obligatory, not optional. And the command is addressed to the whole Christian community. None of us is to get drunk; all of us are to be Spirit-filled. The fullness of the Spirit is not an elitist privilege, but available for all the people of God.

While it is a command, it is a command to allow something to happen to us, not something we are primarily responsible for. The NEB renders it: "Let the Holy Spirit fill you." What is essential is such a penitent turning from what grieves the Holy Spirit and such a believing openness to him that nothing hinders him from filling us.

Instructively, the parallel passage in Colossians reads not "Let the Spirit fill you" but "Let the message of Christ dwell among you richly" (Colossians 3:16). We must never separate the Spirit and the Word. To obey the Word and to surrender to the Spirit are virtually identical.

When are we to be filled? Now. The Greek word describes a continuous action. We are not to be filled just once but to go on being filled. For the fullness of the Spirit is not a one-time experience we can never lose but a privilege to be renewed continuously by continuous belief and obedience. We have been sealed with the Spirit once and for all, but we need to be filled with the Spirit and go on being filled every day and every moment of the day.

Here, then, is a message for both the defeated and the complacent, that is, for Christians at opposite ends of the spiritual spectrum. To the defeated Paul would say, "Be filled with the Spirit, and he will give you a new love, joy, peace, patience, kindness, goodness, faithfulness, meekness, and self-control." To the complacent Paul would say, "Go on being filled with the Spirit. Thank God for what he has given you thus far. But do not say you have arrived. For there is more, much more, yet to come."

Results of Being Filled

Ephesians 5:19-21

> [19]speaking to one another with psalms, hymns, and songs from the Spirit. Sing and make music from your heart to the Lord, [20]always giving thanks to God the Father for

everything, in the name of our Lord Jesus Christ. [21]Submit
to one another out of reverence for Christ.

What are the beneficial results of being filled with the Spirit?
Paul offers four. First, fellowship. "Psalms, hymns and songs
from the Spirit" indicates that the context is public worship.
Whenever Christians assemble, they love to sing both to God
and to each other. Some of the psalms we sing are in reality not
worship of God but mutual exhortation.

Second is worship. "Sing and make music," Paul says, "from
your heart to the Lord." Here the singing is not to one another
but to God. The instruction to sing from your heart has always
given people who are unable to carry a tune much comfort.

A third result of being filled with the Spirit is gratitude (v. 20).
A grumbling spirit is not compatible with the Holy Spirit. The
Spirit-filled believer is full not of complaining, but of thanksgiving.

Although the text reads that we are to give thanks "always
. . . for everything," we must not press these words literally. We
cannot thank God for absolutely everything, including blatant
evil. Of course God's children learn not to argue with him in
their suffering, but to trust him and indeed to thank him for
his loving providence by which he can turn even evil to good
purposes (Romans 8:28). But that is praising God for being
God; it is not praising him for evil. To do this would be to react
insensitively to people's pain and to condone and even encourage evil. God hates evil, and we cannot praise or thank him
for what he despises.

So then the "everything" we are to give thanks to God for
must be qualified by its context; that is, everything "in the name

of our Lord Jesus Christ." Our thanksgiving is to be for all that is consistent with the loving fatherhood of God and the self-revelation he has given us in Jesus Christ. Once again the doctrine of the Trinity informs and directs our devotion. When we are filled with the Holy Spirit we give thanks to God our Father in the name of the Lord Jesus Christ.

The fourth result is submitting to one another. Sometimes a person who claims to be filled with the Spirit becomes aggressive, self-assertive, and brash. But those truly filled with the Spirit always display the meekness and gentleness of Christ. It is one of their most evident characteristics that they submit to one another. They also submit to Christ, for their mutual submissiveness is "out of reverence for Christ."

Such are the wholesome results of the fullness of the Holy Spirit. They all concern our relationships. If we are filled with the Spirit, we will be harmoniously related both to God (worshiping him with joy and thanksgiving) and to each other (speaking and submitting to one another). Spirit-filled believers love God and love each other, which is hardly surprising since the first fruit of the Spirit is love.

Ephesians 5:5-21

....

Discussion Guide

Open

What effectively motivates you in your Christian life?

pleasing God — becoming like Jesus

Study

Read Ephesians 5:5-21.

1. What warning does Paul give in verses 5-7?
   No idolator has place in God's Kingdom

2. In this context what would it mean to be deceived with empty words? *words not from God*

3. Why would Paul call immoral, impure, or greedy people idolaters? *selfish — not pleasing God*

4. In what areas of your life are you most tempted toward idolatry? *food + cooking — pride*

5. Paul contrasts light with darkness to say more about holy living. As light in the Lord, how are we to live (vv. 8-21)? *pleasing God — goodness, righteousness truth*

6. Why is it important that sin is made visible (v. 13)? *We can + need to deal with it*

7. Anything that becomes visible is light. How can Christians transform darkness into light?
   asking help from the LORD to change it — being good ness

8. Note that Paul says, "Be very careful" (v. 15). How can we take care of our Christian life? *— nurture, Bible study, prayer*

9. What are the characteristics of a wise person according to verses 15-17? *Being careful how we live as God desires*

10. Why is it important to make the most of every opportunity? *Time is short - darkness all around*

11. How can we follow the command to "be filled with the Spirit"? *Constantly wanting Him to be in control*

12. What are the beneficial results of being filled with the Holy Spirit (vv. 19-21)? *Joy peace pleasing & thanking the LORD*

13. Why do you think it would be necessary to be filled with the Holy Spirit in order to submit to one another? *Holy Spirit makes us of one mind*

APPLY

1. What differences has Christ's Spirit made in your life?

2. How could you live more wisely?

3. Recommit yourself to God as a child of light. Tell him of your desire to live as such in a dark world and to please him. Ask him to reveal to you sin and idolatry that separate you from him.

9

Ephesians 5:21-33

Love

❧

Authority and Submission

EPHESIANS 5:21

²¹Submit to one another out of reverence for Christ.

The very notion of submission to authority is totally at variance with contemporary attitudes of permissiveness and freedom. What should be our reaction to these liberation movements? As Christians, I do not hesitate to say that we should welcome them. Women, children, and workers have often been suppressed and squashed.

We who name Christ's name need to acknowledge with shame that we ourselves have often acquiesced in the status quo and so helped to perpetuate some forms of human oppression, instead of being in the vanguard of those seeking social change. Women, children, and workers chiefly owe their liberation to Jesus Christ, who treated women and children with courtesy and honor in an age in which they were despised.

We may confidently affirm at least three relevant truths: first, the *dignity* of womanhood, childhood, and servanthood; second, the *equality* before God of all human beings, irrespective of their race, rank, class, culture, sex, or age, because all are made in his image; and the even deeper *unity* of all Christian believers, as fellow members of God's family and of Christ's body (see Colossians 3:11; Galatians 3:28). This is the context in which we consider the following verses.

The submission that Paul calls for from wives, children, and servants is not another word for inferiority. We can make a distinction between persons on the one hand and their roles on the other. Husbands and wives, parents and children, masters and servants have equal dignity as God-like beings, but different God-appointed roles.

Two questions immediately arise about this authority: Where does it come from? And how is it to be used? First, it comes from God. The God of the Bible is a God of order, and in his ordering of human life (such as in the state and the family) he has established certain authority or leadership roles. It is "out of reverence for Christ" that we are to submit to one another.

We have to be careful not to overstate this biblical teaching on authority. It does not mean that the authority of husbands, parents, and masters is unlimited, or that wives, children, and workers are required to give unconditional obedience. No, the submission required is to God's authority delegated to human beings. If, therefore, they misuse their God-given authority, then our duty is no longer conscientiously to submit but conscientiously to refuse to do so. At that point civil disobedience becomes our

Christian duty. As Peter put it to the Sanhedrin: "We must obey God rather than human beings!" (Acts 5:29).

Second, divinely delegated authority must never be used selfishly but always for the benefit of others. Paul warns husbands, parents, and masters against the improper use of their authority, forbids them to exploit their position, and urges them instead to remember their responsibilities and the rights of others.

All those in authority are responsible both to God and to those for whose benefit they have been given it. In a word, the biblical concept of authority spells not tyranny but responsibility.

The Duty of Wives

EPHESIANS 5:22

> ²²Wives, submit yourselves to your own husbands as you
> do to the Lord.

Two reasons are given, or at least implied, for the wife's submission to her husband. The first is drawn from creation and concerns the husband's "headship" of his wife, while the second is drawn from redemption and concerns Christ's "headship" of the church.

The husband's headship is both stated as a fact and made the ground of his wife's submission. But Paul doesn't elaborate on its origin here. For that we turn to 1 Corinthians 11:3-12 and 1 Timothy 2:11-13. In both passages he goes back to Genesis 2 and points out that woman was made *after* man, *out of* man, and *for* man. He adds that man is also born *from* woman, so that man and woman are dependent on one another. Nevertheless, his emphasis is on the order, mode, and purpose of the creation of Eve. And since it is mainly on these facts of creation that Paul bases his case for the husband's headship, his argument has permanent and universal validity, and is not to be dismissed as culturally limited.

The words *submission* and *headship* do not by themselves establish stereotypes of masculine and feminine behavior. Different cultures assign different tasks to men and women, husbands and wives. Nowadays, these conventions are recognized as cultural and are therefore being challenged and in some cases changed.

But the man's (and especially the husband's) headship is not a cultural application of a principle; it is the foundation principle itself. This is not chauvinism but creationism. The new creation in Christ frees us from the distortion of relations between the sexes caused by the fall (Genesis 3:16), but it establishes the original intention of the creation. Jesus himself went back to this beginning (Matthew 19:4-6). He confirmed the teaching of Genesis 1–2.

Turning from biblical revelation to contemporary experience, Christians will agree that our human sexuality is part and parcel of our humanness. Masculinity and femininity represent a profound distinction that is psychological as well as physiological. Of course the sexes are equal before God, but this does not mean they are identical. God himself created man male and female in his likeness. So both equally bear his image, but each also complements the other (Genesis 1:26-27; 2:18-24). The biblical perspective is to hold simultaneously the equality and the complementarity of the sexes.

As we will see in the full context of this passage, both the love of the husband and submission of the wife mean losing oneself that the other may find his or her self—which is the essence of the gospel of Christ. It is also the essence of the marriage relationship, for as the husband loves his wife and the wife submits to her husband, each is seeking to enable the other to become more fully himself and herself.

A Charter for Liberty

EPHESIANS 5:23-24

> [23]For the husband is the head of the wife as Christ is the head of the church, his body, of which he is the Savior. [24]Now as the church submits to Christ, so also wives should submit to their husbands in everything.

We know very well what submission meant in the ancient world. Disdain for women was almost universal. William Barclay sums it up: "The Jews had a low view of women. . . . In Jewish law a woman was not a person, but a thing. She had no legal rights whatsoever; she was absolutely in her husband's possession to do with as he willed. . . . The position was worse in the Greek world. . . . In Rome in Paul's day the matter was still worse." It is against this dark background that Paul's teaching shines with such a bright light.

What then is the nature of the husband's headship in the new society God has inaugurated? To answer we look at Jesus Christ. Although Paul grounds the fact of the husband's headship in creation, he defines it in relation to the headship of Christ the redeemer (v. 23). Christ's headship of his church has already been described in 4:15-16. From Christ as head, the body derives its health and grows into maturity. His headship expresses care rather than control, responsibility rather than rule.

Let me spell out five points that will demonstrate that this is not the blueprint for oppression but rather a charter of genuine liberty.

First, the requirement of submission is a particular example of a general Christian duty. That is, the injunction "wives, submit" (5:22) is preceded by the requirement that we are to "submit to one another" (5:21). If, therefore, it is the wife's duty as wife to submit to her husband, it is also the husband's duty to submit to his wife. Submissiveness is a universal Christian obligation.

Second, the wife's submission is to be given to a lover, not to an ogre. The apostle's instruction is not "Wives submit, husbands boss"; it is, "Wives submit, husbands *love*." Three times the apostle repeats his fundamental charge: "Husbands, love your wives" (5:25); "husbands ought to love their wives" (5:28); "each one of you also must love his wife" (5:33).

Third, the husband is to love like Christ. The pinnacle of this demand is reached in verse 25 where he is exhorted to love his wife "as Christ loved the church and gave himself up for her." This is the totality of self-sacrifice.

Fourth, the husband's love, like Christ's, sacrifices in order to serve. Christ's purpose was to free the church from the spots and wrinkles that mar her beauty. Christian husbands are to have a similar concern. Headship will never be used to suppress one's wife. The husband longs to see her liberated from everything that spoils her true feminine identity.

Last, the wife's submission is but another aspect of love. It is not easy to distinguish clearly between what wives and husbands are to do, submit and love. What does it mean to submit if not to give oneself up to somebody? And what does it mean to love if not to give oneself up for somebody? These are two aspects of the very same thing.

The Duty of Husbands

EPHESIANS 5:25-27

²⁵Husbands, love your wives, just as Christ loved the church and gave himself up for her ²⁶to make her holy, cleansing her by the washing with water through the word, ²⁷and to present her to himself as a radiant church, without stain or wrinkle or any other blemish, but holy and blameless.

We might think that nature itself would teach husbands the priority of loving their wives, but many cultures prove the contrary. Paul uses two analogies to illustrate the tender care that a husband's love for his wife should involve.

The first is that the husband must love his wife as Christ has loved his church. Already in the Old Testament the gracious covenant God made with his people Israel was many times referred to as a marriage, such as in Isaiah 54:5-8. Jesus took over this teaching and boldly referred to himself as the Bridegroom (Mark 2:18-20).

What stands out in Paul's development of this theme is the sacrificial steadfastness of the heavenly Bridegroom's covenant love for his bride. This is what husbands are to imitate. Paul uses five verbs to indicate the unfolding stages of Christ's commitment to his bride, the church. He *loved* her, *gave himself up* for her, *to make* her holy, *cleansing* her that he might *present* her to himself. The words "Christ loved the church," preceding as they do his self-sacrifice on her behalf, seem to look back to his eternal preexistence in which he set his love on his people and determined to come to save them.

He goes on "to make her holy, cleansing her." Perhaps this is a deliberate allusion to the bridal bath that took place before both Jewish and Greek weddings. The cleansing also seems to refer to the initial purification or cleansing from sin and guilt we receive when we first repent and believe in Jesus. It is accomplished by "the washing with water through the word." This is an unambiguous reference to baptism, while the additional reference to "the word" indicates that baptism is no magical or mechanical ceremony, but needs an explanatory word to define its significance, express the promises of cleansing and new life in the Spirit it symbolizes, and arouse our faith.

The heavenly Bridegroom's plan is "to make her holy" (the present process of making her holy in character and conduct by the indwelling Spirit) and finally "to present her to himself" (when Christ returns to take her to himself). She will be radiant. But it also means the radiance of God, the shining forth of his otherwise hidden being. So too the church's true nature will become apparent. On earth she is often in rags and tatters, stained and ugly, despised and persecuted. But one day she will be seen for what she is, nothing less than the bride of Christ.

Christ does not crush the church. Rather he sacrificed himself to serve her, in order that she might become everything he longs for her to be. Just so a husband should never use his headship to crush or stifle his wife, or frustrate her from being herself. His love for her will lead him to an exactly opposite path. He will give himself for her, so that she may develop her full potential under God and become more completely herself.

The Golden Rule

EPHESIANS 5:28-30

[28]In this same way, husbands ought to love their wives as their own bodies. He who loves his wife loves himself. [29]After all, no one ever hated their own body, but they feed and care for their body, just as Christ does the church— [30]for we are members of his body.

After climbing with Paul to these sublime heights of romantic love, many readers sense an anticlimax in verse 28. His instruction to husbands to love their wives seems to descend from the lofty standard of Christ's love to the rather low standard of self-love. This sense of anomaly has led some commentators to try to translate the sentence differently, but their attempts do not succeed because the next sentence stubbornly refuses to convey any meaning but the obvious one: "He who loves his wife loves himself."

The reason is probably that Paul is always a realist. We cannot fully grasp the greatness of Christ's love; it "surpasses knowledge," as he wrote earlier (3:19). Nor do husbands find it easy to apply this standard to the realities of family life. But we all know from everyday experience how we love ourselves. Hence the practical usefulness of the Golden Rule Jesus enunciated: that we should treat others as we would like to be treated (Matthew 7:12).

This exhortation to a husband to "feed and care for" his wife as he does his own body is more than a useful guide to daily behavior, however. It also contains an inner appropriateness, since he and his wife have in fact become "one flesh." God intends sexual intercourse not only to be a union of bodies but to symbolize and express a union of personalities. When husband and wife become deeply one with each other, truly "he who loves his wife loves himself."

This leads the apostle to return in his thought to Christ and so to reach the climax of his argument. So far he has used two analogies for a husband's love of his wife, namely, Christ's loving sacrifice for the church and the husband's loving care of his own body. Now he fuses the two. Christ's bride and Christ's body are the same (see 5:23), "for we are members of his body." He has incorporated us into himself, made us part of himself in a profound, indissoluble union.

A Profound Mystery

EPHESIANS 5:31-33

> [31]"For this reason a man will leave his father and mother and be united to his wife, and the two will become one flesh." [32]This is a profound mystery—but I am talking about Christ and the church. [33]However, each one of you

also must love his wife as he loves himself, and the wife
must respect her husband.

The union of husband and wife described in Genesis 2:24 is "a
profound mystery." Paul begins here by referring to the sacred
depths of sexual union itself. But then he immediately goes on
to its yet deeper symbolism: "I am talking about Christ and the
church." As we saw earlier, a mystery is a revealed truth, and the
profound mystery here is closely akin to that of Jewish-Gentile
unity in the body of Christ (3:2-6). The marriage relationship as
a beautiful model of the church's union in and with Christ. The
three pictures of the church Paul develops in Ephesians—the
body, the building, and the bride—all emphasize the reality of
its unity on account of its union with Christ.

Verse 33 is a succinct summary of the teaching Paul has been
giving to husbands and wives. He began with one couplet: love
and submission. He ends with another: love and respect. The
love he has in mind for the husband sacrifices and serves with a
view to enabling his wife to become what God intends her to be.

Throughout these last paragraphs of Ephesians 5, Paul is not
thinking of what the word *authority* tends to bring to our
minds—power, dominion, and even oppression. This is not at all
the kind of headship the apostle is describing. Certainly,
headship implies a degree of leadership and initiative, as when
Christ came to woo and to win his bride. But more specifically
it implies sacrifice, self-giving for the sake of the beloved, as
when Christ gave himself for his bride. If headship means power
in any sense, then it is power to care and not to crush, to serve
and not to dominate, to facilitate self-fulfillment and not to

frustrate or destroy it. The standard of the husband's love is to be the cross of Christ, on which he surrendered himself even to death in his selfless love for his bride.

Such self-sacrifice is painful. Indeed, love and pain appear to be inseparable, especially in sinners like us, since our fallenness has not been obliterated by our re-creation through Christ. In marriage there is the pain of adjustment, as the old independent *I* gives way to the new interdependent *we*. There is also the pain of vulnerability as closeness to one another leads to self-exposure, self-exposure to mutual knowledge, and knowledge to the risk of rejection. So husbands and wives should not expect to discover harmony without conflict; they have to work at building a relationship of love, respect, and truth.

The giving of oneself to anybody is a recognition of the worth of the other. For if I give myself up, it can only be because I value the other person so highly that I want to sacrifice myself for him or her so that person may develop more fully.

Ephesians 5:21-33

....

Discussion Guide

Open

Why do people value freedom and independence so much?
What can be the downside of freedom and independence?

Study

Read Ephesians 5:21-33.

1. How does verse 21 offer an excellent introduction to this whole passage?

2. Why is the notion of submitting to someone else such a hard one for us?

3. In what ways was Jesus one who submitted?

4. Why would we want to submit to the Lord (v. 22)?

5. The ancient Jewish, Greek, and Roman worlds had a very low view of women, as little more than property with few or no rights. How do verses 22-24 suggest a contrasting picture to that?

6. What do we learn from verses 22-24 about how a wife is to regard her husband?

7. What instructions does Paul emphasize to the husband (vv. 25-33)?

8. How has Christ loved the church?

9. In your own words, what is the husband's goal for his wife (vv. 26-27)?

10. Why do you think it is important for the husband to *love* his wife and a wife to *respect* her husband?

11. How do you respond to the idea that the marriage of believers represents to the world Christ's relationship to his church?

APPLY

1. What would marriages be like if these instructions were followed?

2. If you are a wife, how can your submission to your husband be more like your submission to Christ?

3. If you are a husband, how can you love your wife more like Christ loved the church?

4. How can the Christian community build and support our marriages?

5. If you are married, thank God for the gift of your marriage and the privilege of representing to the world Christ's relationship with his bride. If you are not married, pray for marriages in your community, that they will grow and represent Christ well.

10

Ephesians 6:1-9

Respect

❦

Children, Obey Your Parents

EPHESIANS 6:1

¹Children, obey your parents in the Lord, for this is right.

Paul now addresses parents *and* children. He evidently expects whole families to come together for public worship. That children should have been included in the instructions and given a section of their own indicates the already pervasive influence of him who had said, "Let the little children come to me" (Mark 10:14). It was a radical change from the cruelty toward babies and children that prevailed in the Roman Empire.

He begins with another example of that general submissiveness which according to 5:21 is expected of all members of God's new society: "Children, obey your parents." Although Paul goes on to restrict parental authority and to guide it into the channel of Christian education, it is still clear that parents' authority over their children is distinct from and stronger than the husband's headship over his wife. Yet Paul does not take it for granted. His teaching is always rationally argued.

He begins with nature: "Children, obey your parents, . . . for this is right" or righteous. Child obedience belongs to what medieval theology came to call natural justice. It is no surprise, therefore, when Paul includes disobeying parents as a mark both of a decadent society, which God has given up to its own godlessness, and of "the last days," which began with the coming of Christ (Romans 1:28-30; 2 Timothy 3:1-2).

In addition to nature, he offers another reason for obedience—the gospel and the new day that dawned with Jesus Christ. This is implied in the injunction that children should obey their parents "in the Lord." These words make child obedience a specifically Christian duty, something they are to do because of their own personal relationship to the Lord Jesus Christ.

He as Creator first established order in family and society, and in the new society he is now building he does not overthrow it. Families have not been abolished. What has changed relates to the ravages of the fall. For the family life God created at the beginning and pronounced to be good was spoiled by human rebellion and selfishness. But now "in the Lord," by his reconciling work, God's new society has begun, continuous with the old in the fact of family life but discontinuous in its quality. For now all our relationships are purged of ruinous self-centeredness, and suffused instead with Christ's love and peace.

Even obedience to parents is changed. It is no longer a grudging acquiescence in parental authority. Christian children learn to obey with gladness, "for this pleases the Lord" (Colossians 3:20). Now this same Jesus is their Lord and Savior, and the creator of the new order, so they are anxious to do what pleases him.

Honor Your Parents

EPHESIANS 6:2-3

2"Honor your father and mother"—which is the first commandment with a promise—3"so that it may go well with you and that you may enjoy long life on the earth."

Paul freely conflates the Greek text of Exodus 20:12 and Deuteronomy 5:16. He prefers to enforce God's commandment with a promise than with a threat, a promise concerning material prosperity and long life. Alongside the blessing "in the heavenly realms" (1:3), there is here a promised blessing "on earth." Probably we should interpret this in general rather than individual terms. The promise is not so much long life to each child who obeys their parents, as social stability to any community in which children honor their parents. Certainly a healthy society is inconceivable without a strong family life.

Two practical questions remain. Is the command unconditional? And to whom is it addressed?

Many Christian young people who are anxious to conform their lives to Scripture are perplexed by the requirement of obedience. Are they to obey absolutely everything their parents tell them to do? What if they have come to know Christ but their parents remain unconverted? If their parents forbid them to follow Christ or to join the Christian community, are they obliged to obey? I need first to say that before becoming an adult, obedience to parents should be the norm, and disobedience the rare exception.

For example, suppose a new believer desires to be baptized, but their parents forbid it. I would not advise them to defy their parents' wishes. Baptism can wait until they are older. If, on the other hand, their parents were to forbid them to worship and follow Christ in their heart, this they could not obey. Our loyalty to Christ must come first. If we love our parents more than him, he said, we are not worthy of him. We should never seek family conflict since all the followers of Jesus are called to be peacemakers and, so far as it depends on us, to live peaceably with everybody. Yet sometimes tension simply cannot be avoided.

This brings us to the second practical question: Is Paul addressing himself only to infants and to youth, to those who are under age? No single answer can be given since different answers are needed in different cultures.

In most Western countries people are no longer minors at age eighteen. They can vote and are free to marry without parental consent. However, in some Majority World countries today, especially in Asia, the status of a child continues throughout life until the father dies. Christians should not generally defy the accepted convention of their own culture in this matter. So long as they are regarded in their culture as children or minors, they should continue to obey their parents.

Regardless of age or legal status, we must continue to honor our parents, who occupy a unique position in our lives.

The Duty of Parents

EPHESIANS 6:4

> [4]Fathers, do not exasperate your children; instead, bring
> them up in the training and instruction of the Lord.

The instruction to children to obey their parents presupposes the fact of parental authority. Yet when Paul outlines how parents should behave toward their children, it is not the exercise but the restraint of their authority that he urges on them.

The picture he paints of fathers who are self-controlled, gentle, patient educators of their children is in stark contrast to the norm of his own day, where fathers were autocrats, even killing newborns or enslaving their children if they desired. The overarching theme of Ephesians is that through Christ's reconciling work there is now one multinational, multicultural family of God. So human fathers are to care for their families as God the Father cares for his (3:14-15; 4:6).

Mothers are surely included too. Although the word in verse 4 is *fathers*, it could be used for "fathers and mothers."

Negatively, parents are told: "Do not provoke your children to anger" (RSV). Paul recognizes how delicate a child's personality is. Parents can easily misuse their authority either by making irritating, unreasonable, or harsh demands that make no allowances for the inexperience and immaturity of children. There is a place for discipline, as Paul goes on to say, but it must never be arbitrary. Conversely, almost nothing causes a child's personality to blossom and gifts to develop like the positive encouragement of loving, understanding parents.

Children must be allowed to be themselves. Wise parents recognize this. As Calvin translates it, children are to "be fondly cherished. . . . Deal gently with them."

Regarding instruction, parents should jealously guard their responsibility, delegating some of it to both church and school, but never entirely surrendering it. The Christian upbringing of children is mental as well as moral. Some suggest that parents should be totally nondirective and leave their children to find their own way. Certainly some parents are too directive, too domineering, and thereby inhibit their children from learning to make their own decisions and so grow into maturity. False education is indoctrination; parents and teachers impose their mind and will on the child. True education, on the other hand, is stimulation; parents and teachers act as a catalyst and encourage children to make their own responses. This they cannot do if they leave the child to flounder; they have to teach Christian values of truth and goodness, defend them, and recommend their acceptance, but at the same time abstain from any pressure or coercion.

In all cases, the parents' discipline and instruction is to be "of the Lord." Mothers and fathers must remember that he is their own chief teacher and administrator of discipline.

The Duty of Slaves

EPHESIANS 6:5-8

[5]Slaves, obey your earthly masters with respect and fear, and with sincerity of heart, just as you would obey Christ. [6]Obey them not only to win their favor when their eye is

on you, but as slaves of Christ, doing the will of God from your heart. ⁷Serve wholeheartedly, as if you were serving the Lord, not people, ⁸because you know that the Lord will reward each one for whatever good they do, whether they are slave or free.

Slavery seems to have been universal in the ancient world. A high percentage of the population were slaves. They constituted the work force and included not only domestic servants and manual laborers but educated people as well, like doctors, teachers, and administrators. Slaves could be inherited, purchased, or acquired in settlement of a bad debt. Prisoners of war commonly became slaves. Nobody queried or challenged the arrangement.

To those of us who live in countries where slavery has been abolished, it is hard to conceive how the ownership of one human being by another can have been tolerated. In the Roman Empire slaves had no rights and were often treated cruelly. Even Aristotle could not imagine friendship with a slave. In this context it is immediately remarkable that Paul should address himself to slaves at all, indicating that they were accepted members of the Christian community and that he regards them as responsible people to whom he sends a moral appeal.

In each of these four verses Jesus Christ is mentioned. The Christ-centeredness of this instruction is very striking. The perspective of slaves has changed. Their horizons have broadened. They have been liberated from the slavery of pleasing people into the freedom of serving Christ. Their mundane tasks have been absorbed into a higher preoccupation, namely, "the will of God" (v. 6) and the good pleasure of Christ.

Exactly the same principle can be applied today by Christians in our work and employment. Our great need is the clear-sightedness to see Jesus Christ and to set him before us. It is possible to cook a meal as if Jesus Christ were going to eat it, or to clean the house as if Jesus Christ were to be the honored guest. The presence of Christ is certainly no excuse for bad conditions. On the contrary, it should be a spur to improving them.

Once Christian slaves were clear in their minds that their primary responsibility was to serve the Lord, their service to their earthly masters would become exemplary. First, they would be respectful, obeying them "with respect and fear" (v. 5), which implies not a cringing servility before a human master but rather a reverent acknowledgment of the Lord Jesus, whose authority the master represents.

Next, they would obey "with sincerity of heart" (v. 5), with integrity, without hypocrisy or ulterior motives. Third, they would be conscientious, not only doing it "to win their favor when their eye is on you" but for Christ (v. 6). Fourth, their service would become willing instead of reluctant or grudging. And all this because they know that their Lord is also their judge, and that no good work, whoever does it (slave or free), is ever left unrewarded by him (v. 8).

The Duty of Masters

EPHESIANS 6:9

> [9]And masters, treat your slaves in the same way. Do not threaten them, since you know that he who is both their

Master and yours is in heaven, and there is no favoritism with him.

Although the duties of Christian slaves are spelled out in some detail, Christian slave owners are given only three principles, all of which have far-reaching implications against the background of the middle of the first century AD. First, "treat your slaves in the same way." That is, if you hope to receive respect, show it; if you hope to receive service, give it. It is an application of the Golden Rule. However masters hope their slaves will behave toward them, they must behave toward their slaves in the same way. Paul admits no privileged superiority in the masters, as if they could themselves dispense with the very courtesies they expect to be shown. It is a matter of mutual submission (5:21).

Second, "do not threaten them." As parents are not to provoke their children, so masters are not to threaten their slaves. That is, they are not to misuse their position of authority by issuing threats of punishment. Punishment was accepted in the empire as the only way to keep slaves under control, and Christianity does not deny that in some circumstances punishment is legitimate, even necessary (Romans 13:1-5). But threats are a weapon the powerful wield over the powerless. And a relationship based on threats is not a human relationship at all. So Paul forbade it.

Third, the reason for these requirements is their knowing that Jesus Christ is master of both slave and slave owner, and that "there is no favoritism with him." Slave owners were used to being flattered and fawned upon, but they should not expect (for they will not receive) such discriminatory favoritism from the Lord Christ.

Thus all three principles were designed to lessen the cultural and social gap between slave and slave owner. Instead of regarding his relationship with his slaves as that of proprietor to chattels or of superior to inferiors, he was to develop a relationship in which he gave them the same treatment as he hoped to receive, renounced the unfair weapon of threats, and recalled that he and they both shared the same heavenly master and impartial judge.

The Abolition of Slavery

EPHESIANS 6:9

> ⁹And masters, treat your slaves in the same way. Do not threaten them, since you know that he who is both their Master and yours is in heaven, and there is no favoritism with him.

Before leaving this passage, we must face squarely the topic of slavery and Paul. Did the gospel offer no more radical solution to slavery than an adjustment of personal relationships? Why did Paul not at least command slave owners to emancipate their slaves?

In whatever way we seek to respond, it must never be by condoning slavery. The Christian conscience must condemn slavery in every form. Its evil lies in the ownership by one human being of others, which degrades them. This being so, we again ask why the New Testament did not call for its abolition.

The first answer is the pragmatic one, namely, that Christians were at first an insignificant group in the empire. Their religion was still unlawful, and they were politically powerless. Even if Christians had liberated their slaves, they may have condemned most of them to unemployment and poverty.

Second, in Paul's time slaves regularly became free. According to the results of Tenney Frank's research, between 81 and 49 BC, half a million Roman slaves were freed. This helps to explain both Paul's advice to Corinthian slaves (if they could gain their freedom, to seize the opportunity to do so) and his strong hint to Philemon that he should release Onesimus (1 Corinthians 7:21; Philemon 16).

Third, by that time the legal status of slaves was beginning to be eased and showed signs of further improvement to come. Several emperors introduced liberalizing measures.

This brings us back to how Paul's Ephesian letter transformed the slave-master relationship. First was equality. Nobody at that time could imagine that masters and slaves were equal. Nevertheless, they were equal before God, because they had the same Lord and Judge, who showed no partiality between them (v. 9).

The second quality of their relationship was to be justice, implicit in the general instruction to masters to treat slaves "in the same way." This sounded extremely strange because slaves were still popularly regarded as the property of their masters. And where there are no rights, there can be no justice. So justice for slaves was a revolutionary new concept. Essentially the gospel insisted that slaves had rights.

The third and highest aspect of the transformed slave-master relationship is brotherhood. It appears with conspicuous clarity in Paul's letter to Philemon. The concept of brotherhood was

Paul's innovation. For God's new society is the Father's household or family, all of whose members are related to one another in Christ as brothers and sisters. A message which thus united master and slave as brothers ipso facto issued its radical challenge to this practice, which we must continue to fight even today.

Ephesians 6:1-9

....

DISCUSSION GUIDE

OPEN

What word or phrase would you use to describe your relationship with your parents? Explain.

STUDY

Read Ephesians 6:1-9.

1. How do you see mutual submission (5:21) continuing to be worked out in this passage?

2. What exhortation does Paul give to children (vv. 1-3)?

3. How should this apply to adult children?

4. How are parents to raise their children?

5. What are ways that parents exasperate their children?

6. How can God as our Father be a model for parents?

7. How are Christian slaves to act? Why?

8. What should be the motivation behind the slaves' response to their masters?

9. In that society, what do Christian masters and slaves have in common?

10. How does the theme "for we are all members of his body" (4:25) run throughout this whole section on new relationships (5:21–6:9)?

APPLY

1. If you are a parent, how can you avoid exasperating your children?

2. What implications does this passage have concerning how employers should relate to employees?

3. How can this passage apply to you in your work?

4. Celebrate the body of Christ in which we are all equal. Pray for your brothers and sisters in the Lord for whom you work or who work for you. Ask God to work in your children and to help them to grow in their relationship with him.

11

Ephesians 6:10-24

Power

❧

The Enemy We Face

EPHESIANS 6:10-12

> ¹⁰Finally, be strong in the Lord and in his mighty power. ¹¹Put on the full armor of God, so that you can take your stand against the devil's schemes. ¹²For our struggle is not against flesh and blood, but against the rulers, against the authorities, against the powers of this dark world and against the spiritual forces of evil in the heavenly realms.

In between his summons to seek the Lord's strength and put on God's armor on the one hand (vv. 10-11) and his itemizing of our weapons on the other (vv. 13-20), Paul gives us a full and frightening description of the forces arrayed against us (v. 12). Our struggle is not with human beings but with cosmic intelligences who are demonic.

Paul's original readers were quite familiar with this. They doubtless remembered—or would have heard about—the incident of the Jewish exorcists in Ephesus who were rash enough to try to dismiss an evil spirit in the name of Jesus without knowing Jesus. Instead of succeeding, they were overpowered by the demoniac and fled in panic, "naked and bleeding" (Acts 19:13-17). Encounters like this may have been common since Paul's Ephesian converts had previously dabbled in the occult and then made a public bonfire of their valuable books of magic (Acts 19:18-20).

The forces arrayed against us have three main characteristics. First, they are powerful. Being called rulers and authorities draws our attention to the power they wield.

Second, they are wicked. Power itself is neutral; it can be well used or misused. But our spiritual enemies use their power destructively rather than constructively, for evil not for good. They are utterly unscrupulous and ruthless in the pursuit of their malicious designs.

Third, they are cunning. Paul warns "against the devil's schemes" (v. 11). Because the devil seldom attacks openly, preferring darkness to light, we can be caught unsuspecting when he transforms himself into "an angel of light" (2 Corinthians 11:14). And he is at his wiliest when he succeeds in persuading people that he does not exist.

How can we expect to stand against the assaults of such enemies? It is impossible on our own. Only the power of God can defend us from the might, the evil, and the craft of the devil. God's power raised Jesus Christ from the dead and enthroned him in the heavenly places, and has raised us from the death of sin and enthroned us with Christ. The principalities and powers are working in those same heavenly places (v. 12). So the invisible world from which they attack us and in which we defend ourselves is the very world in which Christ reigns. And we reign with him.

Some Christians are so self-confident that they think they can manage by themselves without the Lord's strength. Others are so self-distrustful that they imagine they have nothing to contribute to their victory in spiritual warfare. Both are mistaken. In verses 10-11 Paul expresses the proper combination of divine enabling ("be strong in the Lord") and human cooperation ("put on the full armor of God"). The power is indeed the Lord's, as is the armor. Without that armor we will be fatally unprotected and exposed, but still we need to take it up and put it on.

The Belt and Breastplate

EPHESIANS 6:13-14

> [13]Therefore put on the full armor of God, so that when the day of evil comes, you may be able to stand your ground, and after you have done everything, to stand. [14]Stand firm then, with the belt of truth buckled around your waist, with the breastplate of righteousness in place.

The purpose for putting on the divine armor is to stand, to be stable. Wobbly Christians who have no firm foothold in Christ are an easy prey for the devil. In the Old Testament, God is depicted as a warrior fighting to vindicate his people by putting "on righteousness as his breastplate, and the helmet of salvation on his head" (Isaiah 59:17). The armor and weapons are his, but now he shares them with us.

Paul details the six main pieces of a soldier's equipment, being very familiar with Roman soldiers. In fact as he dictated Ephesians he was chained to one by the wrist (6:20). And although it would be unlikely that such a bodyguard would wear the full armor of an infantryman on the battlefield, the sight of him close by may well have kindled his imagination.

The first piece of equipment Paul mentions is the belt. Usually made of leather, the soldier's belt was essential. It gathered his tunic together and also held his sword. It ensured that he was unimpeded when marching.

Now the Christian soldier's belt is truth. Many commentators, especially in the early centuries, understood this to mean the revelation of God in Christ and in Scripture. For certainly only the truth can dispel the devil's lies and set us free. Other commentators, however, especially because the definite article is absent in the Greek, prefer to understand Paul to be referring to truth in the sense of integrity. To be deceitful, to lapse into hypocrisy, to resort to intrigue and scheming, this is to play the devil's game, and we will not be able to beat him at his own game.

The second item of the Christian's equipment is "the breastplate of righteousness" (v. 14). The soldier's breastplate often covered his back as well as his front and was the major piece protecting all his most vital organs.

In Paul's letters righteousness more often than not means "justification," that is, God's gracious initiative in putting sinners right with himself through Christ. Certainly no spiritual protection is greater than to be justified by his grace through simple faith in Christ crucified, to be clothed with a righteousness that is not one's own but Christ's, to stand before God not condemned but accepted. This is an essential defense against an accusing conscience and against the attacks of the evil one.

On the other hand, the apostle wrote of moral righteousness in Ephesians 4:24 and 5:9. So the Christian's breastplate may be virtue of character and conduct. For just as cultivating truth is the way to overthrow the devil's deceits, so cultivating righteousness is the way to resist his temptations.

As with the two meanings of truth, we may well combine the two meanings of righteousness since according to Paul's gospel the one would invariably lead to the other.

The Boots and Shield

EPHESIANS 6:15-16

¹⁵and with your feet fitted with the readiness that comes from the gospel of peace. ¹⁶In addition to all this, take up the shield of faith, with which you can extinguish all the flaming arrows of the evil one.

Gospel boots come next in our list of God's armor. Probably Paul is, according to Marcus Barth, referring to the half-boot "of the Roman legionary which was made of leather, left the toes free, had heavy studded soles, and was tied to the ankles and shins with more or less ornamental straps" that "equipped him for long marches and for a solid stance."

The Christian soldier's boots are the gospel of peace. When we have received this good news, we enjoy the firmest possible footing to fight evil from. The phrase could also refer to our "readiness to announce the Good News of peace" (GNT). There can be no doubt that we should always be ready to bear witness to Jesus Christ as God's peacemaker (2:14-15). Such tiptoe readiness has a very stabilizing influence on our own lives, as well as introducing others to the liberating gospel.

For myself I veer slightly toward this second explanation, partly because of the parallel in Colossians 4:5-6 and partly because of the faint echoes of Ephesians 2:17 ("he came and preached peace") and of Isaiah 52:7 ("how beautiful on the mountains are the feet of those who bring good news, who proclaim peace"). In either case the devil fears and hates the gospel, because it is God's power to rescue people from his tyranny. So we need to keep our gospel boots strapped on.

The fourth piece of equipment is "the shield of faith" (v. 16). The word Paul uses does not denote the small round shield that left most of the body unprotected, but the long oblong one, measuring 3.9 by 2.5 feet. It was specially designed to put out the dangerous incendiary missiles then in use, particularly arrows dipped in pitch, which were then lit and fired.

What, then, are "the flaming arrows of the evil one"? No doubt the devil's darts include his mischievous accusations that inflame our conscience with what (if we are sheltering in Christ) can only be called false guilt. Other darts are unsought thoughts of doubt and disobedience, rebellion, lust, malice, or fear.

But there is a shield with which we can extinguish all such fire-tipped darts—"the shield of faith." God himself "is a shield to those who take refuge in him" (Proverbs 30:5), and it is by faith that we flee to him for protection. For faith lays hold of the promises of God in times of doubt and depression, and faith lays hold of the power of God in times of temptation.

The Helmet and Sword

EPHESIANS 6:17

[17]Take the helmet of salvation and the sword of the Spirit, which is the word of God.

The Roman soldier's helmet, which is the next piece of armor on the list, was usually made of a tough metal like bronze or iron. Helmets were decorative as well as protective, and some had magnificent plumes or crests.

"The helmet of salvation" may refer to that measure of salvation we have already received (forgiveness, deliverance from Satan's bondage, and adoption into God's family) or the confident expectation of full salvation on the last day (including resurrection glory and Christlikeness in heaven). Regardless, God's saving power is our only defense against the enemy of our souls. Charles Hodge wrote, "that which adorns and protects the Christian, which enables him to hold up his head with confidence and joy, is the fact that he is saved," and, we might add, that Christians know their salvation will be perfected in the end.

The sixth and last is the sword. Of all the pieces listed, the sword is the only one clearly used for attack as well as defense.

Moreover, the kind of attack envisioned will involve a close personal encounter, for the word used refers to the short sword.

"The sword of the Spirit" is immediately identified as "the word of God." This may well include the words of defense and testimony Jesus promised that the Holy Spirit would put into his followers' lips when they were dragged before magistrates (Matthew 10:17-20). But the expression has a much broader reference than that, namely, to Scripture, God's written Word, whose origin is repeatedly attributed to the inspiration of the Holy Spirit.

It is still his sword, for he still uses it to cut through people's defenses, to prick their consciences and to stab them spiritually awake. Yet he also puts his sword into our hands, so that we may use it both in resisting temptation (as Jesus did, quoting Scripture to counter the devil in the Judean wilderness) and in evangelism. Every Christian evangelist, whether a preacher or a personal witness, knows that God's Word has cutting power, being "sharper than any double-edged sword" (Hebrews 4:12). We must never be ashamed to use it.

Here, then, are the six pieces that make up the whole armor of God: the belt of truth and the breastplate of righteousness, the gospel boots and the faith shield, salvation's helmet and the Spirit's sword. They constitute God's armor, as we have seen, for he supplies it. Yet it is our responsibility to take it up, to put it on, and to use it confidently against the powers of evil. Moreover, we must be sure to avail ourselves of every item of equipment provided and not omit any.

Pray

EPHESIANS 6:18-20

> ¹⁸And pray in the Spirit on all occasions with all kinds of prayers and requests. With this in mind, be alert and always keep on praying for all the Lord's people. ¹⁹Pray also for me, that whenever I speak, words may be given me so that I will fearlessly make known the mystery of the gospel, ²⁰for which I am an ambassador in chains. Pray that I may declare it fearlessly, as I should.

Finally, Paul adds prayer, not (probably) because he thinks of prayer as another weapon, but because it is to pervade all our spiritual warfare. Scripture and prayer belong together as the two chief weapons that the Spirit puts into our hands.

Prevailing Christian prayer has four universals, indicated by the fourfold use of the word *all*. We are to pray "on all occasions" (both regularly and constantly), "with all kinds of prayers and requests" (for it takes many and varied forms), "and always keep on praying" (because we need, like good soldiers, to stay alert and neither give up nor fall asleep), "for all the Lord's people" (since the unity of God's new society, which has been the preoccupation of this whole letter, must be reflected in our prayers).

Perhaps most important is the command to stay alert (v. 18). It goes back to the teaching of Jesus himself. He emphasized the need for watchfulness in view of the unexpectedness of both his return and the onset of temptation (Mark 13:33-37; 14:34-38). "Be watchful" was the general admonition of the apostles because the devil is always on the prowl like a hungry lion, and false teachers like fierce wolves, (and partly because the Lord's return might surprise us) but especially because of our tendency to sleep when we should be praying (1 Peter 5:8; Acts 20:31; 1 Thessalonians 5:1-8; Colossians 4:2). By prayer we wait on the Lord and renew our strength. Without prayer we are much too feeble and flabby to stand against the might of the forces of evil.

"Pray also for me," Paul begged (v. 19). He was wise enough to know his own need of strength if he was to stand against the enemy, and humble enough to ask his friends to pray with him and for him. The strength he needed was not just for his personal confrontation with the devil, however, but for his evangelistic ministry by which he sought to rescue people from the devil's dominion.

Paul asks the Ephesians to pray that he may be given freedom not from confinement but to preach the gospel "fearlessly" (vv. 19-20). He still calls the good news "the mystery" because it has become known only by revelation, and centers on the union of Jews and Gentiles in Christ. He is anxious both to obscure nothing by muddled speech and to hide nothing by cowardly compromise. Clarity and courage remain two of the most crucial characteristics of authentic Christian preaching.

It was for the gospel that he had become "an ambassador in chains" (v. 20). Now what concerns Paul most, however, is not that his wrist may be unchained but that his mouth may be opened in testimony; not that he may be set free but that the gospel may be spread freely and without hindrance. He prays for this and asks the Ephesians to pray too. Against such prayer the principalities and powers are helpless.

Grace and Peace

EPHESIANS 6:21-24

> ²¹Tychicus, the dear brother and faithful servant in the Lord, will tell you everything, so that you also may know how I am and what I am doing. ²²I am sending him to you for this very purpose, that you may know how we are, and that he may encourage you.
>
> ²³Peace to the brothers and sisters, and love with faith from God the Father and the Lord Jesus Christ. ²⁴Grace to all who love our Lord Jesus Christ with an undying love.

Paul has reached the end of his letter. Tychicus will deliver the letter and supplement it with some personal news (vv. 21-22). This no doubt explains the unusual absence at the end of the letter of personal messages and greetings. Tychicus will convey them by word of mouth.

Then there is another reason for the visit of Tychicus to Ephesus and its neighboring cities—to encourage them (v. 22). His exposition of God's new society is no mere theological theory; for he and they are members of it themselves. So they must deepen their fellowship—by praying for one another (1:15-23; 3:14-21; 6:19-20), by his letter to them, and through Tychicus, who would both bring them information about Paul and seek to encourage them. Prayer, correspondence, and visits are still three major means by which Christians and churches can enrich one another and so contribute to the building up of the body of Christ.

It was the custom in the ancient world for correspondents to end their letters with a wish for the reader's health or happiness.

But as Paul has Christianized the opening greeting, so now he Christianizes the final wish. Indeed, what he writes is half wish, half prayer.

Paul's first prayer wish is this for their peace (v. 23), a word that has characterized this letter. He has explained how Jesus Christ "is our peace" since he has broken down the dividing wall and created a single new humanity, "thus making peace." Then he "came and preached peace" (2:14-17). Consequently, Paul begged them to "keep the unity of the Spirit through the bond of peace" (4:3). Paul paints a beautiful picture of the church fellowship and the Christian home pervaded with love and peace, even though no peace treaty can ever be negotiated with the principalities and powers of evil.

Paul's second prayer wish is this: "Grace to all who love our Lord Jesus Christ with an undying love." The apostle began his letter by wishing his readers "grace . . . and peace" (1:2); he now ends it with a similar reference. No two words could summarize the message of the letter more succinctly. For peace in the sense of reconciliation with God and one another is the great achievement of Jesus Christ, and grace is the reason why and the means by which he did it. Moreover, both are indispensable to all members of God's new society.

I venture, then, to make Paul's words my own and offer them as my prayer wish for you, my readers: "Peace to the brothers and sisters. . . . Grace to all who love our Lord Jesus Christ."

Ephesians 6:10-24

....

Discussion Guide

Open

What comes to your mind when you hear the phrase "spiritual warfare"?

Study

Read Ephesians 6:10-24.

1. Look carefully at the description of our enemy in verses 11-12. What do you learn?

2. How does Paul encourage us in verses 10-11 to prepare for battle?

3. Why do you think "standing" is emphasized so much?

4. Which of the six pieces of armor would you find most helpful and why?

5. What do you think are the "flaming arrows of the evil one" (v. 16)?

6. How is prayer to pervade all our spiritual warfare?

7. Why is it difficult to pray the way we are told to pray in this passage?

8. How are the kinds of prayers urged in this passage a continuation of the kind of praying Paul has done throughout the book?

9. What do Paul's final instructions reveal about his relationship with the Ephesians?

10. Paul began his letter by wishing his readers "grace and peace." Now he ends it with a similar reference to grace and peace. Why does Paul focus on these qualities?

APPLY

1. How do you need to shape your prayer life so you can engage in the battle through prayer?

2. How have your goals and desires for your Christian community been influenced by studying Ephesians?

3. Spend time quietly reflecting on the battle and the armor. Ask God to give you wisdom and strength for the battle and to help you to put on the whole armor of God.

Guidelines for Leaders

My grace is sufficient for you.

2 Corinthians 12:9

If leading a small group is something new for you, don't worry. These sessions are designed to flow naturally and be led easily. You may even find that the studies seem to lead themselves!

This study guide is flexible. You can use it with a variety of groups—students, professionals, coworkers, friends, neighborhood or church groups. Each study takes forty-five to sixty minutes in a group setting.

You don't need to be an expert on the Bible or a trained teacher to lead a small group. These guides are designed to facilitate a group's discussion, not a leader's presentation. Guiding group members to discover together what the Bible has to say and to listen together for God's guidance will help them remember much more than a lecture would.

There are some important facts to know about group dynamics and encouraging discussion. The suggestions that follow should equip you to effectively and enjoyably fulfill your role as leader.

PREPARING FOR THE STUDY

1. Ask God to help you understand and apply the passage in your own life. Unless this happens, you will not be prepared to lead others. Pray too for the various members of the group. Ask God to open your hearts to the message of his Word and motivate you to action.

2. Read the introduction to the entire guide to get an overview of the topics that will be explored. *The Message of Ephesians* will give you more detailed information on the text. This can help you deal with answers to tough questions about the text and its context that could come up in discussion.

3. As you begin each study, read and reread the assigned Bible passage to familiarize yourself with it.

4. Carefully work through each question in the study. Spend time in meditation and reflection as you consider how to respond.

5. Write your thoughts and responses. This will help you to express your understanding of the passage clearly.

6. It may help to have a Bible dictionary handy. Use it to look up any unfamiliar words, names, or places.

7. Reflect seriously on how you need to apply the Scripture to your life. Remember that the group members will follow

your lead in responding to the studies. They will not go any deeper than you do.

LEADING THE STUDY

1. At the beginning of your first time together, explain that these studies are meant to be discussions, not lectures. Encourage the members of the group to participate. However, do not put pressure on those who may be hesitant to speak—especially during the first few sessions.

2. Be sure that everyone in your group has a book. Encourage the group to prepare beforehand for each discussion by reading the introduction to the book and the readings for each section.

3. Begin each study on time. Open with prayer, asking God to help the group to understand and apply the passage.

4. Discuss the "Open" question before the Bible passage is read. The "Open" question introduces the theme of the study and helps group members begin to open up, and can reveal where our thoughts and feelings need to be transformed by Scripture. Reading the passage first could tend to color the honest reactions people might otherwise give—because they are, of course, supposed to think the way the Bible does. Encourage as many members as possible to respond to the "Open" question, and be ready to get the discussion going with your own response.

5. Have a group member read aloud the passage to be studied as indicated in the guide.

6. The study questions are designed to be read aloud just as they are written. You may, however, prefer to express them in your own words. There may be times when it is appropriate to deviate from the discussion guide. For example, a question may have already been answered. If so, move on to the next question. Or someone may raise an important question not covered in the guide. Take time to discuss it, but try to keep the group from going off on tangents.

7. Avoid answering your own questions. An eager group quickly becomes passive and silent if members think the leader will do most of the talking. If necessary, repeat or rephrase the question until it is clearly understood, or refer to the commentary woven into the guide to clarify the context or meaning.

8. Don't be afraid of silence in response to the discussion questions. People may need time to think about the question before formulating their answers.

9. Don't be content with just one answer. Ask, "What do the rest of you think?" or "Anything else?" until several people have given answers to the question.

10. Try to be affirming whenever possible. Affirm participation. Never reject an answer; if it is clearly off-base, ask, "Which verse led you to that conclusion?" or again, "What do the rest of you think?"

11. Don't expect every answer to be addressed to you, even though this will probably happen at first. As group members

become more at ease, they will begin to truly interact with each other. This is one sign of healthy discussion.

12. Don't be afraid of controversy. It can be very stimulating. If you don't resolve an issue completely, don't be frustrated. Explain that the group will move on and God may enlighten all of you in later sessions.

13. Periodically summarize what the group has said about the passage. This helps to draw together the various ideas mentioned and gives continuity to the study. But don't preach.

14. Conclude your time together with prayer, asking for God's help in following through on the applications you've identified.

15. End on time.

Many more suggestions and helps for studying a passage or guiding discussion can be found in *How to Lead a LifeGuide Bible Study* and *The Big Book on Small Groups* (both from Inter-Varsity Press).

Reading the Bible with John Stott

- *Reading the Sermon on the Mount with John Stott*

- *Reading Romans with John Stott, volume 1*

- *Reading Romans with John Stott, volume 2*

- *Reading Galatians with John Stott*

- *Reading Ephesians with John Stott*

- *Reading Timothy and Titus with John Stott*

Also Available

The Message of Ephesians